How to
Design
TED-Worthy
Presentation Slides

Presentation Design Principles from the Best TED Talks

Akash P. Karia

Author of the Phenomenal Bestseller,
"How to Deliver a Great TED Talk"

BESTSELLING BOOKS BY AKASH KARIA

Available on Amazon (www.bit.ly/AkashKaria):

How to Deliver a Great TED Talk: Presentation Secrets of the World's Best Speakers

TED Talks Storytelling: 23 Storytelling Secrets from the Best TED Talks

Own the Room: Presentation Techniques to Keep Your Audience on the Edge of Their Seats

How Successful People Think Differently

ANTI Negativity: How to Stop Negative Thinking and Lead a Positive Life

Persuasion Psychology: 26 Powerful Techniques to Persuade Anyone!

Ready, Set...PROCRASTINATE! 23 Anti-Procrastination Tools Designed to Help You Stop Putting Things off and Start Getting Things Done

RAVE READER REVIEWS FOR "HOW TO DESIGN TED-WORTHY PRESENTATION SLIDES"

"Would recommend this book for anyone who does presentations. Very clear and inspiring. **Reading this book changed my presentation style and my slides, both for the better - and I've been a professional speaker for over 30 years.** PowerPoint's take longer to put together now but they're more fun to do and the audience enjoys them better, too."
~ Becki L. James

"**A must read...An essential tool for preparing effective, interesting and "sexy" presentations!** I found it very helpful and well written. I strongly suggest it as a must read for any professional who wants to improve his communicational skills."
~ Rosalinda Scalia

"I will admit to rarely reviewing books. However, **this book was such a step above any others I've read on the art of PowerPoint presentations, I had to give it a five star review.**"
~ David Schwind

"**A great resource!** A great, quick overview of building a strong presentation. I have been teaching workshops at universities and Fortune 500 Campuses up and down the East Coast on building better presentations. Akash hits all the right notes in this book. A must read for anyone wanting to build powerful presentations."
~ David Bishop

"The lessons shared in this short book will a go a long way to helping a person give better public presentations. **The insights shared by Akash are like golden nuggets** in a river full of info!"
~ Alan Portugal

"**Right on the mark. Just what I was looking for as a non-designer.** Quick read hitting all of the items to be considered when designing slides."
~ Erik J. Zettelmayer

"**Excellent for those who want to really engage their audience.** I incorporated many of the principles within and developed a more effective product presentation."
~ Tom Tipps

"**Make a greater impact with your presentations.** While reading this book I was mentally reviewing my talks where I use PowerPoint slides. I am now changing some of those slides to make a greater impact on the listeners. These tips are easy to implement and make sense."
~ John C. Erdman

"As always **we can expect the best from Akash** and we are getting more."
~ Payam Bahrampoor

"This book gives practical advice. However, it does not stop there. **It demonstrates how to use that advice, gives visual examples of what to do and what not to do and explains why.** It turns creating a presentation from a dreaded event to one allowing creativity to flow and your passion about your subject matter to emerge on the screen through your slides."
~ Pandora Training and Consulting

YOUR FREE GIFT

As a way of saying thank you for your purchase, I'd like to offer you a free bonus package worth $297. This bonus package contains eBooks, videos and audiotapes on how to master the art of public speaking, smash through procrastination and triple your productivity. You can download your free bonus here:
http://AkashKaria.com/FREE

A NOTE REGARDING COPYRIGHT

CONTENTS

ACKNOWLEDGEMENTS

I would like to thank my Mum and Dad, Nisha and Paresh Karia, for always being there for me. Thank you Bintee, Chloe, Afshaan, Alfaz, Ali and Salim, for my life is a much prettier picture with you in it.

I would also like to thank the following people, whose work I am heavily indebted to: Eugene Cheng, Sir Ken Robinson, Daniel Pink, Nick Morgan, Becky Blanton, Simon Sinek, Chiara Ojeda, Amy Cuddy, Garr Reynolds, Nancy Duarte, Al Gore, Steve Farnsworth, Nilofer Merchant, Bill Gates, Carmine Gallo, Larry Lessig, Dr. John Medina, Seth Godin, Jacqueline Novogratz, Emiland, Alex Rister, Darren Rowse, Brene Brown, Stuart Firestein, Sebastian Wernick, Rachel Botsman, George Papandreou, Paul Kemp-Robertson, Tim Harford, Douglas Kruger, Pankaj Ghemawat, Dan Pallato, Tim Leberecht, Wolfgang Kessling, Julian Treasure, Guy Kawasaki, and Nic Marks.

I am also heavily indebted to the following organizations: TED, Ethos3, Microsoft Office, Storyful, Harvard Business Review, Slideshare, and Slides that Rock.

Thank you for doing what you do and for inspiring me to write this book!

Akash P. Karia
Author | Speaker | Entrepreneur

AUTHOR'S NOTE ON POWERPOINT

Throughout this book, I make references to using PowerPoint presentations. However, the presentation principles contained within this book are 100% applicable to you even if you are using Keynote or Prezi.

It doesn't matter what presentation software you're using because as long as you follow the proven presentation principles contained within this book, you too can create outstanding slides for your next talk.

Akash Karia

"You can reverse engineer almost any good design. Take apart your favorite presentations, infographics, websites and figure out how it's done and remix it into something new."
~ *Jesse Desjardins*

This book is about studying the best slides from some of the best TED talks, and to reverse-engineer them so that you too can create sexy presentation slides.
~ *Akash Karia*

CHAPTER ONE

BREATHE LIFE INTO YOUR PRESENTATION... INSTEAD OF DRAINING IT OUT OF YOUR AUDIENCE

Examples:

- *Eugene Cheng*
- *Sir Ken Robinson*
- *Daniel Pink*
- *TEDx Speaker Guide*

Have you ever seen a corporate presentation? Isn't it ironic that organizations spend millions of dollars on branding, creating fancy logos and websites to impress customers, but when it comes to creating PowerPoint presentations, many of the presentations are a downright disgrace? They're boring. Dull. Dry. Lifeless.

Let me give you an example. I was recently hired by a well-respected organization to help its employees become better speakers. The moment I walked into the organization's office, I was amazed by how well designed the entire office was – from the comfy red sofas in the visitors lounge, to the plush carpet to the beautiful paintings hanging on the walls. It was obvious that the organization had invested a lot of money to make sure that any client who walked into the office would be impressed.

However, when I met with my workshop participants and looked at the presentations they'd designed (presentations for deals worth millions of dollars), I was horrified. The presentation slides were filled with large chunks of text, against ugly-looking multicolored backgrounds. Would these presentations compel me to do business with the company? Absolutely not!

In my opinion, over 90% of presentations are unbearable. I know because I've made it my life's work to help people stop being terrible presenters. I travel the world giving workshops teaching people how to be better presenters. I talk to CEOs and executives, and what I find is that they invest heavily on advertisement and logo design, but they usually have a very small or no budget set aside to train their employees on how to become more engaging speakers.

Source: Eugene Cheng

Every day, audience members are forced to sit through mind-numbing, text-heavy, data-filled presentations that end up doing more damage than good.

Have you ever sat through such a presentation?

Have you ever given one?

For a TED talk (*http://www.TED.com*), presenters are given a maximum slot of 18 minutes to share their message with the world. Some choose to present without slides. For example, Sir Ken Robinson delivered a very inspiring speech on education without the use of any slides (*www.AkashKaria.com/Ken*). He felt that his talk didn't require any visual aids, so instead of using slides as a crutch (which is what most mediocre presenters do) he gave his talk without them.

Other presenters, however, choose to use slides to help promote the understanding of their message. The important point here is this: They used the slides to help amplify the understanding of their message.

Instead of relying on the slides as a crutch and using them as blown-up versions of notecards to help them remember what they had to say, the effective speakers on the TED stage used to slides to help their audience, not themselves.

For example, consider how in his TED talk on "The surprising science of motivation," Daniel Pink (*www.AkashKaria.com/Dan*) used the visual in the slide below to help his audience understand an experiment called "the candle problem." Notice how the primary objective of the slide was to help his audience, not him:

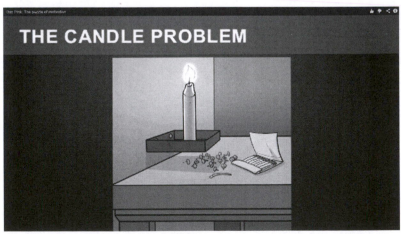

Source: Daniel Pink via TED

So here's the first key takeaway from the book. When designing your slides, ask yourself:

Am I including this slide to help my audience or to help myself?

If your slide doesn't help your audience, then don't include it in your presentation. Effective presentations are always about the audience, never about the speaker. This may sound like a very simple and obvious point, but its effectiveness cannot be overstated.

According to the TEDx speaker guide, which is available for free on the Internet (*http://bit.ly/TEDXGuide*):

> Slides can be helpful for the audience, but they are by no means necessary or relevant to every talk. Ask yourself: Would my slides help and clarify information for the audience, or would they distract and confuse them?

If your slides help clarify the information for your audience, include them. If not, and if you're using the slides as a crutch, then forget about the slides.

*

Because a TED talk is such an important event, some of the speakers pay big bucks to hire famous presentation design firms to design their slides for them. You might not have the budget to hire a design firm to create your visuals. Or you might not *want* to hire someone else to design your slides for you and prefer to create the visuals yourself. Whatever the case, this guide will serve as a crash course on how to create highly effective and visually pleasing slides that grab and keep your audience's attention.

WHY YOU MIGHT NOT WANT TO BUY THIS BOOK

This guide is not meant to be a complete primer on presentation design. However, it does cover the essentials of presentation design. I've kept the book short because I know you're a busy person and I don't want to waste your time with fluff. Inside the book you'll find examples of sexy presentation slides from great TED talks, along with actionable principles you can use to make your own presentations come alive.

Even though this guide isn't a complete primer on presentation design, implementing the principles covered in this book will make your presentations better than 90% of speakers – in other words – your presentations will be in the top 10% of presentations given.

This should be enough for you to deliver awesome presentations, but if you'd like to get into a lot more nitty-gritty principles, such as how to use Photoshop to edit images to be used in your slides, then I'll point you to some other great resources where you can get hold of such information.

However, the principles covered in this book will satisfy the majority of presenters. If you're looking for very advanced tips on presentation design (such as how to use Adobe Photoshop and Illustrator to make your images sexier), then you should probably look elsewhere. This isn't a book on how to use software; it's a short book that outlines basic guidelines for effective presentation design.

WHY SHOULD YOU CARE ABOUT PRESENTATION DESIGN?

At this point, you might be asking yourself, "Why do I need to spend time making my PowerPoint slides look beautiful? If my audience understands my message, who cares if my slides are crappy?"

Nowadays, it's not enough to just display bullet points on the screen. The advice of having six bullet points with six words in each bullet is old and outdated. It results in a boring presentation.

Unfortunately, your audiences judge you and your talk on the quality of your slides. If your slides are high quality and beautifully designed, your audience will be enthusiastic about listening to you. However, if your slides are badly designed, they'll think to themselves, "If he didn't spend much time on designing his slides, it's likely that he didn't spend much time in preparing his talk either."

In other words, badly designed slides give your audience the impression that you don't care about them. Once they develop a negative perception of you, it'll be very difficult to get your audience interested in you and your message.

Is it possible to give a great presentation despite crappy slides?

Yes, it's possible.

However, you'd have to be a brilliant speaker in order to overcome the negative perception your slides have created. It's much easier to learn how to create effective and engaging slides instead.

HOW THIS BOOK IS STRUCTURED

This book is structured into three parts. The first part briefly talks about the message of your talk because no matter how beautifully designed your presentation slides are, if your message sucks, your presentation will suck.

The second part is where you will find the real meat of the book. You will discover universal presentation design principles you can use to create effective and sexy slides that help you communicate your message instead of distracting from it.

Finally, the third part focuses on key principles for delivering your slides in a dynamic and engaging manner. Again, this section is not covered in great detail because that is not the aim of this book. However, if you are interested in what to say in your TED talk and how to say it, I would recommend checking out my first book in this series, How to Deliver a Great TED Talk (*www.AkashKaria.com/TEDTalkBook*).

MAKE YOUR SLIDES WORK <u>FOR</u> YOU

The aim of this guide is not only to help you create sexy slides, but also to help you create *effective* ones that promote the understanding of your message. Slide design isn't about making your slides look pretty. It's about eliminating clutter, promoting simplicity and enhancing the effectiveness of your message.

Of course, doing all these things will result in a more visually appealing slide. Whether you're giving a TED talk or a business presentation, you'll learn simple presentation design principles to make your slides work *for* you and not against you.

If you follow the principles in this guide, I guarantee that you'll be able to create slides that help you breathe life into your presentations instead of draining it out of your audience.

Let's get started...

PART 1

YOUR MESSAGE

- The most common mistake – and how to avoid it.
- The one principle that will make you better than 90% of most speakers.

CHAPTER TWO

THE MOST COMMON MISTAKE – AND HOW TO AVOID IT

Examples:

- *Nick Morgan*
- *Becky Blanton*
- *Simon Sinek*
- *Chiara Ojeda*

One of the most common mistakes most presenters make is that the moment they realize they have to deliver a presentation, they immediately open up PowerPoint or Keynote and start dumping their information onto the slides. The result is a very dry and lifeless presentation that is filled with too much text and too little inspiration.

Instead, the first thing I recommend you do is find your core message. The core message refers to the single most important idea you want your audience to take away from your presentation. What is the one single idea you want your audience to remember?

Nick Morgan, who has coached many TEDx speakers, writes in his blog post on "How to Deliver a 20-Minute TED-Like Talk" (*http://bit.ly/18lF6ww*):

> "Begin by choosing one idea. Try to make it an idea that has universal interest, but where your specific expertise can usefully be applied. Then, narrow it down and focus it..."

Becky Blanton, who presented at TEDGlobal 2009, emphasized the importance of selecting a core message in an article she wrote for Six Minutes (*http://bit.ly/244tM*). In her article titled *"How to Deliver the Talk of Your Life,"* she wrote:

> "Convey one strong idea. Take time to focus each idea you want to express, then pick the most compelling, the strongest idea."

Let's look at some examples of core messages from TED talks:

Watch Simon Sinek's TED talk here: *www.AkashKaria.com/Simon*

What was the core message of Simon's talk?

Did you get it?

It's hard to miss.

Simon's core message was "start with why." Those three words can summarize his entire talk. Of course, there were several other important points he brought up in his presentation, but "start with why" was the core message of his speech. All the other points were supporting ones.

Simon didn't use slides in his TED talk, but one of my favorite presentation designers, Chiara Ojeda (*http://slidesha.re/12FNcl1*), created a Slideshare presentation around the talk. As illustrated in Chiara's slide below, the core message of the talk was "start with why":

Source: Chiara Ojeda

You should be able to write your core message in less than ten words. If your core message is not crystal-clear to you, it won't be clear to your audience. Ask yourself:

"If my audience was to forget everything else I said what one single message would I want them to remember?"

In Dan Pink's TED talk, the core message of the speech was that motivation is not about "[enticing] people with a sweeter carrot or [threatening] them with a sharper stick. We need a whole new approach." All the examples, research and stories used in Dan's talk were used to support his core message.

The core message of your presentation is of vital importance because it helps you decide what to keep in and what to toss out. Perhaps you have a great story, or example or statistic you want to include in the presentation.

Should you include it or toss it?

If it backs up your core message, keep it.

If not, toss it.

It may be great, but it doesn't belong in this presentation. As a result, your final presentation will end up being very clear and laser-focused.

IN A NUTSHELL

- Avoid the temptation of dumping all your information onto your slides.

- Convey only one key message.

- Write your core message down in less than ten words.

CHAPTER THREE

THIS ONE PRINCIPLE WILL MAKE YOU BETTER THAN 90% OF PRESENTERS

Examples:

- *TEDx Speaker Guide*
- *Simon Sinek*
- *Amy Cuddy*

In 2008, I attended a recruitment talk by a Fortune 500 company in Hong Kong. I, along with 20 other people in the room, was there to learn about the exciting opportunities of working with the company.

On that day, the speaker began her presentation in the following manner (names and dates have been changed):

> "Our company was founded in 1769. It started off as a one-man firm and then grew into a 20-man operation. After that, we merged with Company XYZ, and our operations expanded into 26 countries. We now have over 20,000 employees

and our annual revenue exceeds X million dollars..."

The PowerPoint slide that the speaker had displayed on the screen was a vertical timeline of the company's growth from 1769 to 2008. For the next 20 minutes, she waded through the entire history of the company, outlining all the acquisitions the company had made. I was bored to death. I tried to stifle my yawns, but I noticed that several others in the room weren't as polite and at least three people had fallen asleep slumped in their chairs.

I see this mistake all the time when I attend corporate presentations. Presenters talk about "I – I – I." Their presentations are too "I-focused," when really they should be "you-focused." They should be about the audience, not about the speaker and the company. If you're talking about yourself and your company, you're definitely doing the wrong thing.

The solution is pretty simple: Make your presentations you-focused. This is one of the guidelines included in the TEDx speaker guide:

"Don't focus too much on yourself."

To elaborate on this guideline, this means that you should be using a lot more you-related words ("you," "your," "you're") than I-related words ("I," "me"). Talk about the audience, not yourself! For example, consider this you-focused opening from Simon Sinek's brilliant TED talk, "Start with Why."

Notice how the you-focused opening immediately grabs the audience's attention:

> "How do you explain when things don't go as we assume? Or better, how do you explain when others are able to achieve things that seem to defy all of the assumptions? For example: Why is Apple so innovative? Year after year, after year, after year, they're more innovative than all their competition."

Let's consider another you-focused section from Simon's talk:

> "People don't buy what you do; they buy why you do it. And if you talk about what you believe, you will attract those who believe what you believe. But why is it important to attract those who believe what you believe? Something called the law of diffusion of innovation, and if you don't know the law, you definitely know the terminology.
>
> The first two and a half percent of our population are our innovators. The next 13 and a half percent of our population are our early adopters. The next 34 percent are your early majority, your late majority and your laggards. The only reason these people buy touch tone phones is because you can't buy rotary phones anymore."

Did you notice how many you-focused words Simon had in his speech? He was constantly relating his talk to his audience. The focus was on his audience, not on himself.

To exhaust this point, let's have another look at another TED speaker who gave a you-focused presentation. Let's have a look at the opening from Amy Cuddy's TED talk, "Your body language shapes who you are" (*www.AkashKaria.com/Amy*):

> "I want to ask you to right now do a little audit of your body and what you're doing with your body. So how many of you are sort of making yourselves smaller?
>
> Maybe you're hunching, crossing your legs, maybe wrapping your ankles. Sometimes we hold onto our arms like this. Sometimes we spread out. (Laughter) I see you. (Laughter) So I want you to pay attention to what you're doing right now.
>
> We're going to come back to that in a few minutes, and I'm hoping that if you learn to tweak this a little bit, it could significantly change the way your life unfolds."

I won't go into much more detail regarding presentation content, because that is already heavily covered in the book, *How to Deliver a Great TED Talk*. However, to summarize, all the great TED speakers that I've watched deliver you-focused presentations. They constantly use you-focused questions and statements to relate their presentation back to the audience.

Why?

Because ultimately presentations are about the audience, not the speaker. If you understand and apply this one simple principle, your presentations will be better than 90% of most presentations.

IN A NUTSHELL

- I-focused presentations will bore your audience.

- Focus on your audience, not on yourself.

- Use you-focused language to keep your presentation relevant to your audience.

PART 2

YOUR SLIDES

- The first step to creating TED-worthy slides
- How to quickly storyboard your presentation
- How to transform slides from dull to dashing
- Is it OK to use 200 slides in 18 minutes?
- The Seth Godin presentation formula
- Are your fonts sexy enough?
- The importance of contrast
- Displaying data without being dull
- Spicing up your presentations with video
- Ensuring consistency between slides

CHAPTER FOUR

THE FIRST STEP TO CREATING TED-WORTHY SLIDES

Examples:

- *Garr Reynolds*
- *Nancy Duarte*
- *Microsoft Office*

Have you ever seen a slide that was crammed with too much text?

One that contained full, grammatically correct sentences?

And all the presenter did was read those sentences out loud while facing the slide?

Newbie presenters often fall into the trap of cramming everything into one slide. The reason they fall prey to this trap is because they idea-dump on their slides instead of idea dumping on paper. The moment they hear the words, "You have to give a presentation," they automatically open up PowerPoint or Keynote and write down all their ideas on their slides.

Sometimes, they copy-paste entire paragraphs off Word documents and into their slides. The result is terrible a "slideument" (a word invented by presentation guru Garr Reynolds) – a cross between a Word document and a PowerPoint slide that succeeds as neither.

So, here's the first rule for creating effective slides: Do your idea-dumps on paper. Grab a clean sheet of paper and a pen (remember those non-techy tools?) and jot down all your ideas and key points. This is the brainstorming part of your presentation.

Write down all the ideas that come to mind.

Don't hold anything back.

Don't judge your ideas.

Simply write them down.

Source: dumbledad via Compfight

On her blog, presentation expert and bestselling author of *Slide:ology* Nancy Duarte has a post called *"Use a Brainstorm before you open PowerPoint"* (*http://bit.ly/15OuGr3*). Nancy's presentation design firm created the slides for Al Gore's presentation and feature film, "An Inconvenient Truth." Anyway, in her blog, she writes about the benefits of brainstorming:

> "Whether it's an official-'cause-its-on-my-calendar brainstorm…or a "quickstorm" (a spontaneous 20-30 minute all-out cram session with some of the brightest folks you work with) collecting perspectives early on can be an enormous help."

Even the Microsoft Office website (*http://bit.ly/15QTz5r*) encourages the use of brainstorming:

> "Brainstorming is an effective method for generating ideas and creatively solving problems."

Next, it's time to pick only the best ideas from your brainstorm. Select only a couple of key ideas – the ones that are essential to your core message. These are the ideas that you should feature in the presentation. Get rid of everything else.

IN A NUTSHELL

- Don't create slideuments!

- Begin with a brainstorm.

- Select only a couple of key ideas to support your core message.

CHAPTER FIVE

HOW TO QUICKLY STORYBOARD YOUR PRESENTATION

Examples:

- *Nancy Duarte*
- *Steve Farnsworth*
- *Eugene Cheng*
- *Harvard Business Review*
- *Nilofer Merchant*

Once you've found your core message, done an idea-dump on paper, selected a couple of the points you would like to elaborate upon and organized them into a logical, easy to follow, step-by-step sequence, it's time to storyboard your presentation.

Notice how, so far into the presentation process, we haven't even opened up PowerPoint or Keynote. We're doing everything the old-fashioned way, using pen and paper, getting our ideas and presentation flow on paper before we start designing the actual slides.

The advantage of doing things on paper is that we aren't restricted by the sequential format of a piece of software such as PowerPoint or Keynote. Nancy Duarte, who gave the TED talk, "The secret structure of great TED talks" (*http://bit.ly/yrDGfo*), was interviewed for the TED blog (*http://bit.ly/SkUByj*). When asked, "What is the best way to start creating a presentation?" she said:

> "My best advice is to not start in PowerPoint. Presentation tools force you to think through information linearly, and you really need to start by thinking of the whole instead of the individual lines. I encourage people to use 3×5 note cards or sticky notes — write one idea per note. I tape mine up on the wall and then study them. Then I arrange them and rearrange them — just work and work until the structure feels sound."

I, along with hundreds of other presentation experts, have found that for some reason ideas seem to flow better when we're sketching them out on a piece of paper as opposed to doing things on a computer. I suspect that one of the reasons might be because sketching engages our right brain – the motion of sketching ideas on a piece of paper spurs our creativity – which results in more ideas that we can choose from.

In any case, after you've organized the points you'd like to elaborate upon in your presentation, it's time to storyboard your presentation. What is a storyboard? It's a visual outline of your presentation:

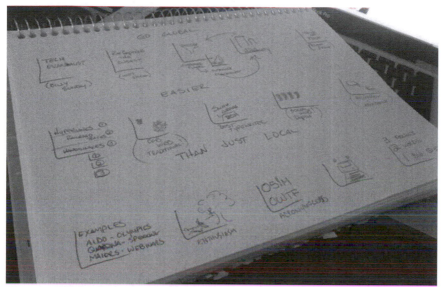

Source: Mike Sansone via Compfight

Storyboards were first used for movies, but their use has extended to marketing, advertising and presentation design. Why are they used in presentation design? Because they free presenters from the self-imposed constraints of using headings and bullet points.

By default, presentation software such as PowerPoint pushes presenters into using boring, standard templates, which limits the creativity of the presentations. It's much better to free yourself from the creativity-limiting constraints of software, step away from the computer, and storyboard your presentation using pencil, pen and paper.

THE BEST METHOD FOR STORYBOARDING

The best way to storyboard is to grab a bunch of sticky notes. Each sticky note represents a slide in your presentation. Next, quickly sketch a visual representation of your idea on the slide.

Steve Farnsworth, a Forbes Top 50 social media influencer and an advisor to the TEDxSanJoseCA event, writes in a blog post titled "How to Make Your Presentation Wow Like a TED Talk" (*http://blog.eloqua.com/ted-talks*):

> "If you have to use slides, keep it simple-stupid. Just a clean visual representation or picture is best. A word or two per slide if you must."

For your storyboard, sketch out visual representations of your ideas on your slides. The visual representation could be charts, graphs, pictures, photos, etc., that you will use in your slides.

So, why should you bother with storyboarding your presentation anyway?

Eugene Cheng, a professional presentation designer based in Singapore, writes in his blog about the benefits of storyboarding. The main benefit, he says, it that storyboarding allows you to know to save time because you know what you will be working on (*http://bit.ly/16NwJst*):

> "Most people tend to jump right into working on PowerPoint without carefully considering what they would be working on or about. As a result, their judgments are clouded by the array of features offered in slide-ware and they have to almost guess what their next slide would be. Most of the times, a substantial amount of time is wasted and deadlines are not met as a result. Worse still, the audience is unable to receive the best presentation that could have been given."

At this point, you might be saying, "I'm convinced about the benefits of storyboarding, but I don't know how to sketch!"

It's okay.

Your sketches are supposed to be rough sketches. They're *not* supposed to be masterpieces. We're not looking for a perfect piece of artwork. All we're looking for is a simple sketch that allows you to transfer your ideas from your head and onto the paper.

You don't have to be an artist to create storyboards. Even stick figures are fine, as long as you manage to get a rough illustration of what you would like on your slides.

As much as possible, avoid using text and instead try to represent your idea visually because visuals are much more interesting, engaging and memorable than text.

According to the Harvard Business Review blog (*http://bit.ly/18lqPnZ*), using sticky notes for storyboarding is great because "the small space forces you to use simple, clear words and pictures. Limit yourself to one idea per slide: There's no reason to crowd them. This sketching process will help you clarify what you want to say and how you want to say it."

The other advantage of using sticky notes for storyboarding is that you can stick the notes up on the wall and examine the sequence and flow of your presentation. You can change the order and check to see if a different arrangement works better. You can experiment with different slides and arrangements until you find a flow that works best for your presentation.

Nilofer Merchant *(www.AkashKaria.com/Nilofer)*, who has graced the TED stage along with speakers such as world-famous rock star Bono, wrote the following in her article "Secrets from a TED2013 Speaker: Preparing for the 'Talk of One's Life'" *(http://linkd.in/15B0dwh)*:

> "Many people start with slides and PowerPoint to map out their talk. What is better is if you know the high-level story arc of the talk, what stories should follow what other stories, and so on...the key no one really tells you is this: only after you've

conceptualized everything, write the script or PPT."

Your storyboard will help you conceptualize your talk. By the end of the storyboarding exercise, you will have sketched out the intended flow of your presentation as well as the intended visuals for your slides. Having done this, the rest of the presentation design process becomes much easier. You now have a rough idea for what your final presentation will look like.

All you have left remaining is to locate the right visuals and fonts so that you can design the actual slides.

IN A NUTSHELL

- Presentation software limits your creativity.

- Use a storyboard to map out your talk.

- Create visual representations of your ideas.

CHAPTER SIX

BILL GATES: DULL TO DASHING SLIDES

Examples:

- *Bill Gates*
- *Craig Valentine*
- *Carmine Gallo*
- *Amy Cuddy*

When transferring your key points from paper and onto slides, remember that you should limit the amount of text on your slides.

This means that you should only use keywords. If your slides contain complete sentences, you're definitely heading down the wrong path.

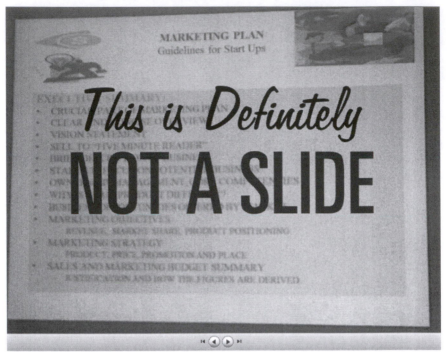

Source: Eugene Cheng

Here's the problem with text-heavy slides:

- **They quickly tire your audience's eyes** and send your audience members to sleep.

- **They create the temptation of reading word for word.** If your slides contain complete sentences, it's difficult for even professional presenters to avoid the temptation of reading the text word for word. As professional speaker Craig Valentine says, "If you and your slides are saying the same thing, one of you is not needed."

- **Audience can't concentrate on you.** If you have a lot of text on your slides, your audience's attention is going to be divided. Should they listen to you or should they read the text on your slides? While you're busy explaining the first bullet point, they've already jumped onto the third one. If you've written everything they need to know on the slide, they already know what you're going to say and no longer need to listen to you. According to the TEDx speaker guide, "Use as little text as possible – if your audience is reading, they are not listening."

- **They are boring and uninspiring.** Let's face it: Text-heavy slides are anything but inspiring. They're deadly dull.

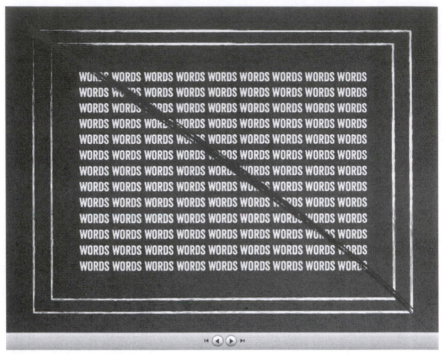

Source: Eugene Cheng

Make sure your slide contains only keywords because having a lot of text on screen tires your audience's eyes and sends them to sleep. A bullet point on screen should not explain the idea... it should only represent it.

This all may seem like common sense, but it's definitely not common practice. Why? One of the reasons is that many presenters double their slides as handouts.

However, this should not be the case. If your slides can double as handouts, it means you're doing something wrong. It means that you have way too much text on your slides.

Don't be lazy: Don't double your slides as handouts. Put in the effort to create a proper set of handouts for your audience.

BILL GATES: DULL TO DASHING SLIDES

In his *Windows Live* presentation, Bill Gates used some very ugly, bullet-filled slides to launch Windows Live. Take a look at a sample slide from the presentation:

Source: niallkennedy via Flickr

Apart from the background being highly distracting, there are too many bullets and too many words on the screen. The slide looks like it's been created by a ten-year-old, without much thought being put into its design. The slide is boring and that in turn makes Windows Live look boring.

Would you be inspired to buy or use Windows Live after looking at such a slide?

Probably not.

Fortunately, Bill Gates has learned that your slides can make or break a presentation.

Carmine Gallo, author of 'The Presentation Secrets of Steve Jobs', writes in an article on BusinessWeek.com (*http://buswk.co/bVH7fA*):

> "I was particularly surprised by one speaker in the 2010 [TED] conference—Bill Gates. The former Microsoft CEO was never known for visually simple slides while he ran the giant software company he co-founded. But as Gates has transformed into a global advocate for helping the world's poor, his presentations have evolved, with more photographs and less text."

In his 2010 TED talk, Bill Gates used highly visual slides to deliver his message. (Watch the talk here: *www.AkashKaria.com/Bill*)

Check out the slide below from Bill's TED talk:

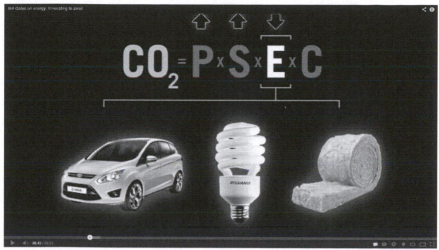

Source: Bill Gates via TED

Notice how this slide is not at all cluttered like the previous one. It contains very little text and no bullet points.

It doesn't distract the audience and leaves the audience free to concentrate on what Bill has to say.

Every one of the TED speakers I watched followed the rule of minimizing text on slides. Here is another example of a great slide used in a TED talk by Amy Cuddy that follows the rule of minimizing text on slides (next page). In fact, there is *no text* at all!

Source: Amy Cuddy via TED

Next time you design a slide for your TED talk (or for any other presentation or speech), make sure you limit the amount of text on your slide.

IN A NUTSHELL

- Text-heavy slides are boring.

- Minimize text on slides.

- Sometimes no text is the best option.

CHAPTER SEVEN

200 SLIDES IN 18 MINUTES

Examples:

- *Nancy Duarte*
- *Larry Lessig*

Another reason many presenters cram a lot of text into their slides is because they feel that they need to limit the total number of slides they have in a presentation. This is complete nonsense. There is no presentation rule that says you have to limit your slides to a certain number!

You should include as many slides as you need in a presentation. Don't cram a lot of points into one slide because of some nonexistent rule. Instead, include only one main idea per slide.

Believe it or not, your audience members have a difficult task – they have to absorb everything you're saying, while also making sense of your slides. If you have complex slides that contain a lot of text and a lot of points, you're making it very difficult for your audience to stay interested in your presentation.

Instead of displaying a cluttered, complex slide that tries to cram all your information into one slide, break your presentation down into a series of different slides with each slide dealing with only one idea or point.

On Nancy Duarte's blog (*http://bit.ly/1dsQJGr*), she writes:

> "During a live presentation, visuals exist in time as well as space. The audience doesn't need to stare at the same four points while the speaker weaves his story around each of them. So we turned this single bullet slide into four different slides, letting the audience absorb them one at a time and (once again) highlighting the speaker's voice as the most important part of the experience."

So, is there a limit to how many slides you should use? Absolutely not.

LARRY LESSIG: 200 SLIDES

In his TED talk on "How creativity is being strangled by the law," Professor Larry Lessig (*www.AkashKaria.com/Larry*) used 200 slides. Yes, you read that correctly: 200 slides for an 18-minute TED talk. For example, let's take just one sentence from Larry's talk:

> "1906. This man, John Philip Sousa, traveled to this place, the United States Capitol, to talk about this

technology, what he called the, quote, 'talking machines.'"

When delivering that one sentence, Larry used three slides! Let's look at the slides and how he used them (*Images: Larry Lessig via TED*):

"1906. This man, John Philip Sousa..."

"... traveled to this place, the United States Capitol..."

"... to talk about this technology, what he called the, quote, 'talking machines'..."

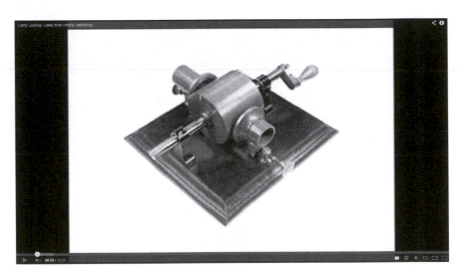

Three slides for one sentence!

However, notice how the effectively the slides were used. By displaying a picture of John Philip Sousa, Larry quickly got the audience familiar with him so that they could follow along with the rest of the story.

The slide displaying a picture of the "talking machines" is also very effective because it avoids the complication of having to explain what the technology looked like. Again, seeing a picture of the technology allows the audience to follow along with the story without needing elaborate explanations.

This just proves the point – use as many slides as you need, but only as long as your slides help your audience. Your slides should never be used as a crutch, only as aids to help your audience understand your story and your talk better.

Still not convinced? Why should you follow the "one idea = one slide" rule? Because it:

- **Eliminates clutter.** Following the one idea per slide rule eliminates clutter. Instead of cramming a lot of different ideas and points into one slide, you have a cleaner, simpler slide that deals with only one point.

- **Keeps your audience's attention on you.** The problem with having a lot of points on one slide is that your audience members read faster than you talk. Therefore, they will be reading while you are talking, meaning that they won't be paying attention to you.

- **Keeps your audience curious.** Let's say you are giving a presentation on "five reasons most people never achieve their dreams." If you have one slide that contains all five points on the slide, your audience already knows what you're going to say. Hence, no curiosity. Instead, keep your audience curious about what you're going to say by only dealing with one idea per slide.

- **Gives you room to include large, visually stunning images**. At most, you will have only one line of text on your slide. This gives you enough room to include a large image or a chart that hammers home your point. Using images not only helps your audience remember your points, but it also helps you create a slide that is pleasing to look at.

Overall, the one idea per slide rule helps you create slides which are clutter-free, keeps your audience curious and engaged, and gives you room to include visually stunning images.

IN A NUTSHELL

- Focus on eliminating clutter.

- Use as many slides as you need.

- One slide = one idea.

CHAPTER EIGHT

THE SETH GODIN PRESENTATION FORMULA

Examples:

- *Dr. John Medina*
- *Seth Godin*
- *Dan Pink*
- *Al Gore*
- *Jacqueline Novogratz*
- *Emiland*
- *Alex Rister*
- *Darren Rowse*
- *Nancy Duarte*
- *Brene Brown*
- *Stuart Firestein*

If you want to create sexy slides for your TED talk, it is essential that you use large, visually stunning images in your presentation. Not only do pictures make your slides look sexier, they also increase the memorability of your presentation.

According to research presented in the brilliant book *Brain Rules* by Dr. John Medina, three days after a presentation, most people only remember approximately 10% of what they heard. However, if you add a picture, recall shoots up to 65%.

THE SETH GODIN PRESENTATION FORMULA

In his TED talk, "Why tribes, not money or factories, will change the world" (*www.AkashKaria.com/Seth*), Seth Godin's slides consisted of many large, colorful images with almost no text on them. His audience could process the image within milliseconds, allowing them to then fully concentrate on what Seth was saying. Here's a sample slide from Seth's talk:

Source: Seth Godin via TED

The images in Seth's slides served as a visual anchor for what Seth was saying.

What do I mean by visual anchor?

A visual anchor is an image that hooks the point you are making to your listener's memory. It helps your audience remember the point by providing a visual representation of that point.

When creating your next presentation, consider using the Seth Godin presentation formula: Fill up your slides with large pictures and very little or no text. Use the images to serve as visual anchors for what you are saying.

USE IMAGES TO MAKE IT EASIER FOR YOUR AUDIENCE TO UNDERSTAND

Visual aids are exactly that – *aids*. They aid your audience's understanding of the topic. Your images should help your audience understand your topic better. For example, if you are describing a very complicated process, then using an image of the process is a good idea to make it easier for your audience to understand what you are saying. In fact, whenever you are trying to explain anything complicated, using an image to help describe it is a good idea.

For example, in his TED talk "The science of motivation," Dan Pink was describing an experiment that was conducted. While the experiment wasn't overly complicated, explaining the setup without a picture would take too much time and might be confusing. Therefore, Dan had a slide that was filled up by an image that showed the experiment setup:

Source: Daniel Pink via TED

The image aids the understanding of the message because seeing the experiment setup makes it very clear to the audience how the experiment works. The visual, combined with Dan's explanation of the visual, makes the experiment setup very clear to the audience:

> "This is called the candle problem. Some of you might have seen this before. It's created in 1945 by a psychologist named Karl Duncker. Karl Duncker created this experiment that is used in a whole variety of experiments in behavioral science. And here's how it works. Suppose I'm the experimenter.

I bring you into a room. I give you a candle, some thumbtacks and some matches. And I say to you, "Your job is to attach the candle to the wall so the wax doesn't drip onto the table." Now what would you do?"

When you have to describe a process, an experiment or any kind of complicated relationship between different objects, try to see if you can use a simple image to help your audience understand it better.

REPRESENT THE IDEA VISUALLY

Have you heard the cliché, "An image is worth a thousand words"? It's a cliché because it's true. Usually, a single image will convey an idea better than several paragraphs of text.

When creating your slides, ask yourself, "Can what I am trying to say be demonstrated visually using a picture?" If it can, then ditch the text and use an image instead.

For a short lesson on how an idea can be represented visually, check out this great Slideshare presentation that walks you through the process: *http://slidesha.re/16iCyOi*

CHOOSE IMAGES THAT CREATE AN EMOTIONAL RESPONSE IN YOUR AUDIENCE

When choosing images for your presentation, choose images that arouse an emotional response in your audience. The best presentations arouse the audience's emotions. Using powerful images is an easy way to arouse your audience's emotions.

Here's a simplistic example. If you are giving a presentation on homelessness, instead of using a picture of a group of homeless people standing outside a shelter, use a picture of an old woman sitting hunched under a tree, holding up a piece of cardboard to protect herself from the rain. The picture of the old homeless woman is going to arouse stronger emotions in your audience than the picture of a mass of people standing outside a homeless shelter.

How do you know which image is going to arouse your audience's emotions? Here's the guideline: Choose the image that creates the largest emotional response in you. If the image arouses your emotions, it will arouse your audience's.

I remember watching Al Gore's presentation on climate change. His documentary had a very powerful impact on me. One of the reasons that his presentation was so powerful was because he used images that aroused powerful emotions in his audience.

For example, when talking about global warming, he used pictures of polar bears drowning as the ice underneath their feet melted. Images such as these aroused sympathy for the fate of the polar bears. It caused me to *care* for the polar bears, and in turn, it caused me to care about global warming. That's the power of emotional images!

Source: Flickr

Unfortunately, Al Gore's TED talk on global warming was not as impressive.

His slides consisted of text-only, and while his talk made sense on an intellectual level, it failed to involve the viewer on an emotional level.

Check out the sample slide from Al Gore's TED talk, "Averting the climate crisis" (*www.AkashKaria.com/Gore*):

Source: Al Gore via TED

When you are trying to persuade people to change their views on a topic and get them to behave differently, you must appeal to their emotions.

People make decisions based on emotions, and then justify their actions using logic. Don't just make intellectual arguments – also arouse your audience's emotions using powerful images.

USE PHOTOS FROM YOUR PERSONAL COLLECTION

Where can you find visually arresting images that arouse your audience's emotions?

You can buy photos from stock photography sites such as *www.stockphotos.com*. Alternatively, you can use *www.compfight.com* to search for images with a Creative Commons license. If you're going to use images that have a Creative Commons license, make sure you give the author of the image appropriate credit for their work.

According to TED:

> "You must properly license all images for TED's use in worldwide video and web distribution (we may use the images in TEDTalks, which are distributed globally for free). Don't grab images from the web. Use high-resolution pictures and graphics. Full-quality photos from a digital camera will look better than images pulled off the web."

A third alternative is to use photos that you have taken. If you have taken some high-quality digital images that are aesthetically pleasing and relevant to the point you are making, consider using them in your presentation.

For example, in her TED talk about escaping poverty, Jacqueline Novogratz displayed photos of a slum she visited in Kenya (*www.AkashKaria.com/Jacqueline*). The photos made the situation much more real for the audience and helped them understand the poverty in Kenya because they could see proof of it.

Source: Jacqueline Novogratz via TED

No matter where you decide to get your photos and pictures (whether from stock photo websites or from your personal collection), there are several important things to keep in mind:

- Use high-quality photographs.
- Don't grab random images off the web because it might result in copyright issues.
- Never stretch a small image to fit your slide because it will result in a low quality, pixelated image.

THE THREE-SECOND RULE

The three-second rule states that your audience should understand your slide within three seconds of seeing it. Therefore, use images that are simple and clearly represent your point. Your slide should be like a billboard – it should contain a large image that grabs your audience's attention and it should be understood easily and quickly.

Source: Emiland via Slideshare

According to Alex Rister, founder of Creating Communication (*http://bit.ly/KyOO9e*):

> "Your slide should pass the three-second rule of glance media. Consider billboard advertising. If an automobile driver can't process that billboard in three seconds, he or she a) won't digest or act on the advertisement and b) will probably wreck the car trying to read more than three seconds of information.
>
> Think of your audience as those drivers. If it takes them more than three seconds to process your slide, you're wrecking their chances of processing and acting on the material you're presenting."

FULL-BLEED IMAGES

When using images, make sure you use full-bleed images. What does it mean to bleed the image? This simply means that the image takes up the entire slide. Here's an example:

Image on slide: Chris Yarzab via Compfight

Full-bleed images are more appealing to look at than thumbnails of pictures placed on slides, such as the one below:

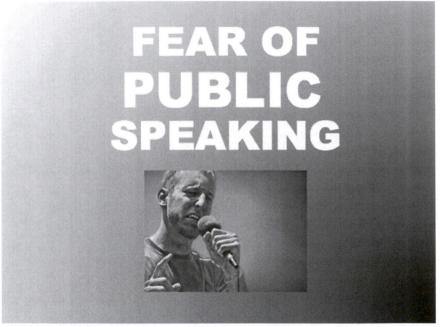

Image on slide: Chris Yarzab via Compfight

A final advantage of filling up your slide with a visually stunning picture is that it creates variety between slides so that audiences do not get tired of the same, repetitive background.

THE RULE OF THIRDS

Images are most powerful when they follow the rule of thirds. What is the rule of thirds? The rule of thirds refers to dividing a slide into thirds (both horizontally and vertically) as follows:

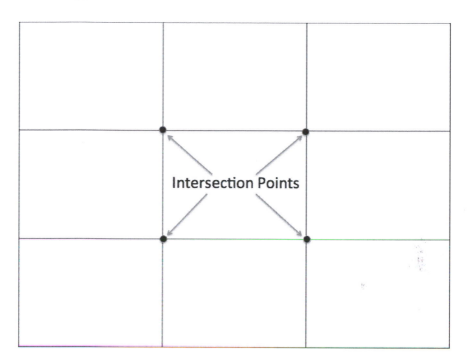

According to the 'Digital Photography School' blog run by Darren Rowse (*http://bit.ly/1evHSXB*), here's why the rule of thirds is useful:

> "The theory is that if you place points of interest in the intersections or along the lines that your photo becomes more balanced and will enable a viewer of the image to interact with it more naturally. Studies have shown that when viewing images that people's eyes usually go to one of the intersection points most naturally rather than the center of the shot –

using the rule of thirds works with this natural way of viewing an image rather than working against it."

Here's an example of an image that uses the rule of thirds to create visual appeal:

Source: Eugene Cheng

Notice how the subject has been placed along the line (at the point of intersection), which is more interesting than having the subject placed in the center of the image. Plus, having the image positioned this way allows you to use the remaining space to add text.

So, how do you know if you're positioning the image according to the rule of thirds? Fortunately, PowerPoint has a feature that allows you to view the grids on slides by following these instructions (Source: *http://bit.ly/19l6H2u*):

"1. On the Home tab, in the Drawing group, click Arrange, point to Align, and then click Grid Settings.

TIP: You can also right-click an empty area of the slide (not a placeholder) or the margin around the slide, and then click Grid and Guides.

2. Under Guide settings, select the Display drawing guides on screen check box."

Using gridlines will make it easier for you to align your images according to the rule of thirds. These gridlines will also help you align all the elements on your slides (images, text, data), giving your slides a clean, well-organized and sleek look."

AVOID CLICHÉD IMAGES

The image you use must be new and fresh. What do I mean by new and fresh? There are some images which have been used so often that they have become clichés.

For example, presenters have overused the image of the handshake to represent teamwork or collaboration. It's an obvious image, and it is *boring!* If your audience is forced to stare at an overused image, they're going to tune out of your presentation. Instead, find a new, exciting and fresh way to represent the idea visually.

Nancy Duarte, in her Q&A with the TED blog, said it best. I think that the following is one of the *best* pieces of advice I have heard about choosing non-cliché images:

> "[For visuals], I think people tend to go with the easiest, fastest idea. Like, "I'm going to put a handshake in front of a globe to mean partnership!" Well, how many handshakes in front of a globe do we have to look at before we realize it's a total cliché?
>
> Another common one — the arrow in the middle of a bull's eye. Really? Everyone else is thinking that way. The slides themselves are supposed to be a mnemonic device for the audience so they can remember what you had to say. They're not just a teleprompter for the speaker. A bull's eye isn't going to make anyone remember anything.
>
> Don't go for the first idea. Think about the point you're trying to make and brainstorm individual moments that you're trying to emphasize. Think to the second, the third, the fourth idea — and by the time you get to about the tenth idea, those will be the more clever memorable things for the audience."

As Nancy says, the imagery you use should be exciting. Let me give you an example. I live in Africa. If I was asked to speak on the topic of teamwork, I might use a high quality, visually stunning image of a pack of lions hunting together. Of course, I would stick to the same theme, using pictures of African wildlife, to make sure that all my slides are visually consistent and have the same theme.

Since I live in Africa and many of my audience members have probably gone on safari, this image would work well for my presentation. You, however, would have to find another image that works well for you. The point here is this: Avoid clichéd images. Find new and exciting ways to represent your idea visually.

UTILIZE THE POWER OF EMPTY SPACE

What you leave out of a slide is just as important as what you put on it. Great designers know the power of empty space. Empty space isn't just something to be filled. Instead, empty space gives balance to the different elements on your slide. It allows breathing room between the different elements. It creates a sense of balance and naturalness.

Unfortunately, a lot of presenters don't appreciate the power of empty space. They fill their slides up with as many different elements as possible – logos, pictures, text, graphs, charts. The result is a slide that is too cluttered and noisy. Cluttered slides quickly tire the eyes and send your audience members to sleep.

Don't be tempted to fill your entire slide up. Instead of cluttering your slides up with lots of images, text, logos and charts, allow your slides to breathe. For example, check out the slide on the next page from Brene Brown's TED talk on "The power of vulnerability" (*www.AkashKaria.com/Brene*).

Notice how the slide contains a simple image, only two words and plenty of empty space. It's a simple, non-cluttered slide, which is what makes it visually appealing:

Source: Brene Brown via TED

Here's another slide from Brene's talk:

And finally, check out this slide from Stuart Firestein's TED talk (*www.AkashKaria.com/Stuart*), which contains a large image and plenty of empty space:

07:21 / 18:34

Source: Stuart Firestein via TED

Learn to appreciate empty space. Ask yourself, "What elements can I eliminate on this slide without compromising the effectiveness and message of the slide? Which elements on this slide are nonessential?"

Get rid of all nonessential elements – text, logos, legends on graphs – and create enough empty space on your slides to give them a natural sense of balance.

IN A NUTSHELL

- Use large, visually stunning images as anchors to help your audience remember your points and arouse their emotions.

- Avoid clichéd images.

- Use the rule of thirds to make your slides more interesting.

- Utilize the power of empty space.

CHAPTER NINE

IS YOUR FONT SEXY ENOUGH?

Examples:

- *CERN*
- *Chiara Ojeda*
- *Sebastian Wernicke*
- *Slides that Rock*
- *Eugene Cheng*
- *Rachel Botsman*
- *George Papandreou*
- *Paul Kemp-Robertson*
- *Bill Gates*
- *Tim Harford*
- *Douglas Kruger*

The discovery of the Higgs boson particle (also known as the "God particle") is one of the greatest discoveries of our time. Scientists at the European Organization for Nuclear Research (CERN) announced the discovery of this groundbreaking particle using a PowerPoint.

Even though this was a very important discovery, the PowerPoint used to announce it was laughable. The font used was Comic Sans (no pun intended). Because the PowerPoint was so poorly designed (and the font choice was terrible), it failed to convey the groundbreaking significance of the particle and inspired ridicule instead of awe. Check out a sample slide here:

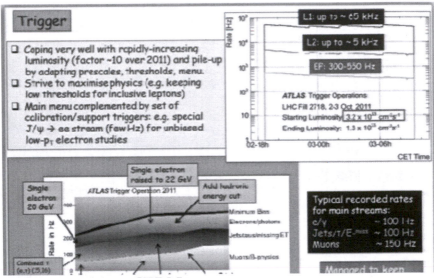

Source: Storyful via CERN

The point of this story? Your PowerPoint is an integral part of your talk. If you quickly put together some slides without paying attention to design and font choice, your presentation might end up being inducted into the "PowerPoint Hall of Shame."

We've agreed that you should limit the amount of text on your slide, but when you do use text, it is important you use the right font. You might not think that font choice is important, but the fonts you choose can have a big impact on the success of your presentation. **The different shapes and sizes of fonts give the fonts different personalities, and these personalities affect the audience's emotions on an unconscious level.**

Image on slide: Chiara Odeja

CHOOSE A FONT THAT MATCHES YOUR MESSAGE

You might not realize it, but different fonts convey different feelings. Fonts have personalities. Some fonts are reserved for serious presentations, whereas other fonts can be used for lighthearted presentations. Consider the font in my slide below:

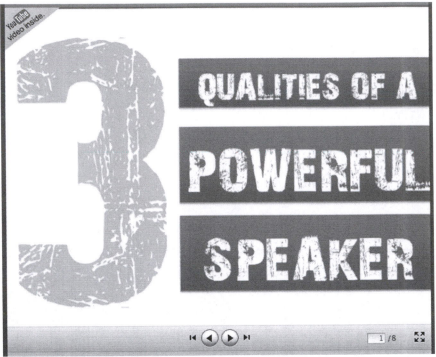

Source: Akash Karia via Slideshare

What feelings does the font in the above slide convey? Some words that come to mind are: Bold. Powerful. Commanding. Authoritative. Impactful.

Consider an alternative font in the slide below.

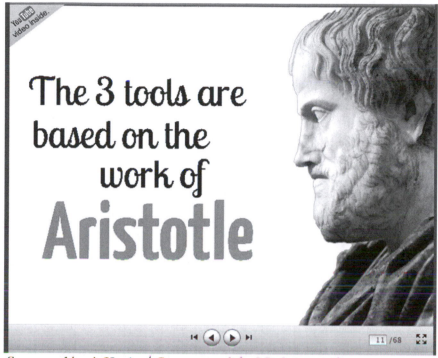

Source: Akash Karia / Image on slide: Nick in exsilio

What feelings does this font convey? Some words that come to mind are: Elegant. Sleek. Sophisticated. Stylish.

Since different fonts convey different feelings, it's important you choose a font that matches your message. Your typeface must be congruent with your message. What kind of feeling are you trying to convey? Try out different fonts until you find a font that matches the mood you are trying to create.

For example, in his TED talk called "Lies, damned lies and statistics (about TED talks)" Sebastian Wernicke (*www.AkashKaria.com/Sebastian*) shared with the audience his statistical analysis on how to create the optimum TED talk. The talk was fun and lighthearted. Thus, he chose a font that would convey this mood. Check out a sample slide from his TED talk:

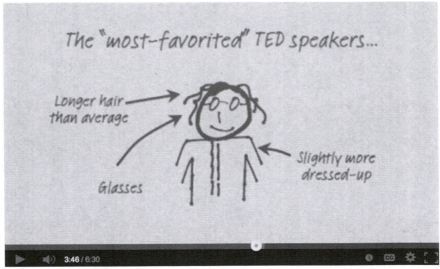

Source: Sebastian Wernicke via TED

The typography in Sebastian's slides perfectly matches the mood he is trying to create: The handwriting-style font gives the impression that the slides are notes from Sebastian's analysis. At the same time, the font is such that it lets the audience know this is not a serious, academic-type analysis, but rather a fun, lighthearted one.

What do the fonts say about your presentation? What mood does the typography on your slides create?

Don't be limited by the fonts that come pre-installed on your computer. Treat the font as a graphic – it is a visual element of your presentation, much like an image. It contributes to the overall look and feel of your presentation, so make sure that you choose a font that matches the tone of your presentation while also being aesthetically pleasing.

You don't have to choose the same old Times New Roman font every time you present. Instead, look around on the Internet. Google the term "free fonts" and you will find hundreds of websites offering free fonts for download.

STICK TO TWO FONT TYPES

If you're just discovering new fonts on the Internet, it might be tempting to go crazy and use as many different fonts as you can. There are so many awesome fonts online that you might feel the urge to use as many as you can. However, this is not a good idea. Simplicity and consistency are the keys to a good presentation. Thus, don't use too many fonts.

Stick to only two fonts – one that you use for extra-large text to draw attention to it by making it stick out, and one for smaller-sized text. For example, on the title slide, you could use one font type for the title and another font size for the subheading.

When pairing different fonts together, make sure that you choose fonts that have similar personalities. Mixing a serious and professional font with a font such as Comic Sans results in a personality clash. The mixed font personalities send a confusing message about your presentation. When using more than one font for your presentation, make sure you use fonts with personalities that complement each other.

If you aren't sure which fonts complement each other, go to *www.Slideshare.net* and browse around some of the presentations. When you find a presentation that uses a combination of fonts that you like, take a screenshot of one of the slides and upload it to *http://www.whatfontis.com/*. This will generate a list of similar free and commercial fonts that you can download and use in your presentation.

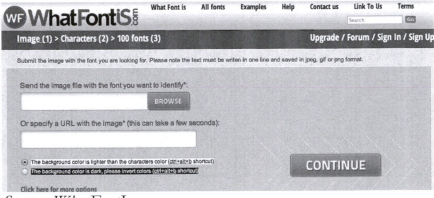

Source: WhatFontIs.com

For example, while browsing around on Slideshare, I was inspired by a presentation designed by the presentation design firm *Slides that Rock:*

Source: Slides that Rock via Slideshare

Using *http://www.fontis.com*, I was able to find the combination of the fonts used in one of their presentations: Tungsten for the primary font and Reklame Script for the smaller, secondary font.

Three other websites where you can download more awesome free fonts are:

- *www.1001freefonts.com*
- *www.dafont.com*
- *www.fontsquirrel.com*

Don't just stick to the boring old fonts on your computer. Be creative. Browse around on the Internet for font combinations that look good together and which convey the right mood for your presentation.

Here's one important point to note when choosing fonts. Try to use fonts that contain a large family.

What do I mean by font family?

Font family refers to the different font options available: condensed, regular, bold, italic, etc. At the very least, make sure that the font you are downloading has a regular, bold and italic version available. This larger the font family, the more options you have at your disposal to create a visual hierarchy within the same font.

So, here's the key takeaway: Don't just look at fonts as a way of putting text up on the screen. Instead, see font types as an essential element that adds to the overall visual appeal of your presentation.

Side note: It's important that you embed all new fonts into your presentation software, otherwise they won't display properly on other computers. Another option would be to save your presentation as a PDF.

DESIGN FOR THE PERSON SITTING AT THE BACK OF THE ROOM

When designing your presentation, design it for the person sitting at the back of the room. This means that your font size should be large enough for the person sitting furthest away from you to read clearly. If people have to struggle to read what you've written, they're going to stop trying and you're going to lose their attention.

Source: Eugene Cheng via Slideshare

For example, look at the slide below, taken from Rachel Botsman's TED talk (*www.AkashKaria.com/Rachel*) called "The currency of the new economy is trust." On the slide, Rachel displays a quote by Mark Pagel. Look at how large the font is to ensure that it is clearly readable from the back of the room:

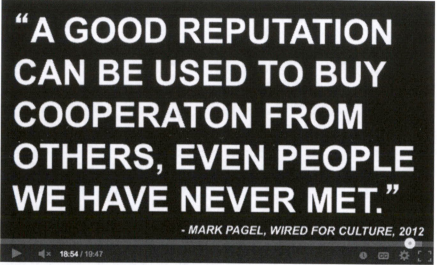

Source: Rachel Botsman via TED

Think of your slides as billboards. Your audience should be able to read what's on your slide/billboard from far away, even if they're driving.

Source: Eugene Cheng via Slideshare

VARY FONT SIZES TO CREATE EXCITEMENT

Using different font sizes on a single slide is a great way of building visual hierarchy. Let's say that you are displaying a quote on the screen. In this case, you could make your text impactful by making the most important keyword in the quote the largest part of the text. This helps your audience get the point of your slide immediately because one element of your design is clearly the dominant one.

For an example, look at the slide below from George Papandreou's TED talk, "Imagine a democracy without borders" (*www.AkashKaria.com/George*):

Source: George Papandreou via TED

As George's slide shows, font sizes can be used to show the relative power, importance and relationship between two ideas.

In the slide on the next page from Paul Kemp-Robertson's TED talk (*www.AkashKaria.com/Paul*), notice how font size is used to draw attention to the most important element of the slide:

Source: Paul Kemp-Robertson via TED

If you pay attention to billboards and other forms of advertising, you'll see this same principle in action:

Source: Thomas Hawk via Flickr

Varying font sizes ensures that your typography is not monotonous and boring. It adds excitement and variety to your typography, making your text sexier to look at.

Small caveat: Like with all principles covered in this book, the key to creating a sexy presentation is balance. Don't go overboard with any of the techniques in this book. Two different font sizes on a single slide are usually enough. Any more and you might end up confusing your audience and making it difficult for them to read your slides.

PAY ATTENTION TO ALIGNMENT

Alignment is an important principle of design. When an audience member looks at your slide, all the elements on it should look like they're placed with thought and care.

Here's an example (next page) of a good slide from Bill Gates' TED talk (*www.AkashKaria.com/Bill*) where all the images and text on the slide are aligned and connected:

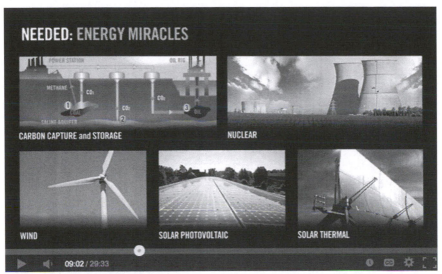

Source: Bill Gates via TED

The image below shows how the invisible lines in the slide above connect the headline, the five images on the slide and the captions beneath the images. The dotted lines in the image represent the "invisible lines":

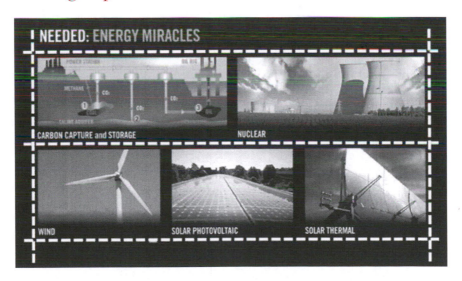

The principle of alignment is also visible in good advertisements. Let's have a look at the KFC ad again, and this time pay attention to the alignment of the text. Notice how the text is left-aligned, giving the ad a clean, organized look:

Source: Thomas Hawk via Flickr

Finally, let's have another look at the slide by Paul-Kemp Robertson where the text is centrally aligned and you can picture an invisible line running vertically through the center of the slide:

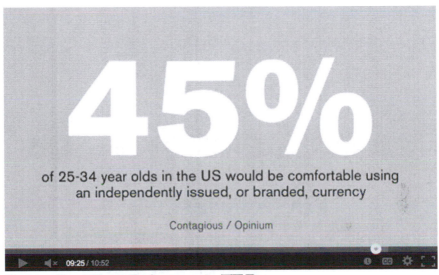

Source: Paul Kemp-Robertson via TED

When creating slides for your TED talk, make sure that you pay attention to these invisible lines so that there is a visual connection between all the elements on your slide. Use the grids on your PowerPoint to make sure that all the elements on your slide are aligned. You should be able to draw the invisible lines and see the connection between all the elements.

PROXIMITY

When different elements on the slide belong together, they should be placed in close proximity to each other. Let's have a look at an example where no thought has been placed regarding proximity and line spacing between text elements:

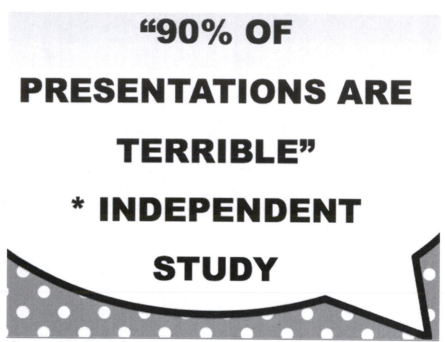

Source: Akash Karia via CommunicationSkillsTips.com

In the slide above, there are two main elements – the quote and the source of the quote. The fact that all the lines of text are spaced equally far apart makes each line seem like a separate element. Hence, it takes a while for the audience members to digest the information on the slide.

Let's change the slide so that the quote and the quote source are clearly two different elements. We will do this by changing the proximity between the lines. Furthermore, we will change the font sizes so that the most important elements on the slide are clearly visible, whereas the less important elements are given less emphasis. Here's how the slide would look:

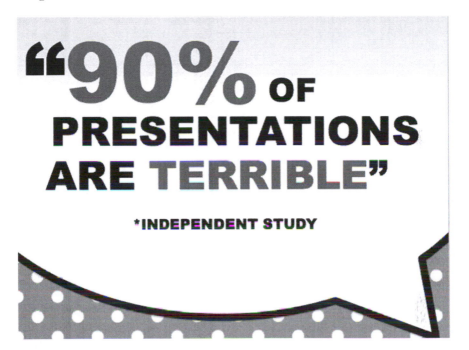

Source: Akash Karia via CommunicationSkillsTips.com

While this isn't a brilliant slide, notice how much better it is than the previous one. The quote and the source are clearly two different elements, and the spacing between them has been adjusted so that the slide is easier to read.

Let's have another look at the TED talk slide by Paul-Kemp Robertson, which pays attention to the principle of proximity to clearly separate the quotation from the source:

Source: Paul Kemp-Robertson via TED

Here's another example from Paul's talk:

While this may be a simplistic example, it proves the point that line spacing and proximity are two very important design principles you should keep in mind when creating your slides.

To adjust the line spacing on PowerPoint, you can go to *Format >> Paragraph >> Line Spacing Options*

Alternatively, you can write each line of text in a separate text box. After that, you can manually move the text boxes closer or further apart. This allows you the freedom to customize the spacing between the lines so you can create the look you desire.

EXPERIMENT WITH ROTATING TEXT

A final way to add excitement to your typography is to experiment with rotating text. What do I mean by that? Here's an example of rotated text from George Papandreou's TED talk:

Source: George Papandreou via TED

In George's slide, the text was slightly rotated clockwise to illustrate the relative weights of democracy and power and wealth.

However, you can rotate text simply for aesthetic purposes. Here's an example of a great book cover that grabs attention using rotated text:

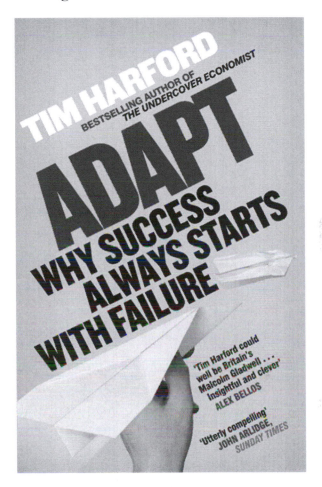

Source: Adapt by Tim Harford

Here's another example from a promotional video for a DVD training course. The DVD is by one of my favorite speakers, Douglas Kruger (*www.DouglasKruger.com*). Look at how the text is slightly rotated to make it interesting:

Source: Douglas Kruger via Wedding Friends

Rotating your text slightly makes your text more exciting to look at. People pay attention to uncommon things, and rotated texts are definitely uncommon. Consider adding a slight rotation to your text to make your typography more exciting.

Once again, balance is the key to success. Use this technique, but don't go crazy with it. Use it, but use it sparingly. Having too much rotating text on your slides makes your audiences dizzy (I know because when I first started designing slides, I made this mistake).

Plus, if you rotate text on every single slide, it becomes predictable and people don't pay attention to predictable things.

IN A NUTSHELL

- Choose a font that matches your message.

- Stick to a maximum of two fonts per presentation.

- Design for the person sitting at the back of the room.

- Vary font size to create excitement.

- Experiment with rotating text.

- Pay attention to alignment.

CHAPTER TEN

"DUDE, WHERE'S THE CONTRAST?"

Examples:

- *Pankaj Ghemawat*
- *Garr Reynolds*
- *Bill Gates*
- *Dan Pallato*
- *Jesse Desjardins*
- *Tim Leberecht*
- *Wolfgang Kessling*

We've talked about fonts, but what about backgrounds? What kind of background should you use?

After studying over 200 TED talks, I have found that the best backgrounds are the ones that are the simplest. Using a simple background keeps your text readable. Aim for a solid color for the background because this allows you to create a clean slide.

A clean slide allows your audience to focus on the text as opposed to being distracted by a busy background. You may, however, use a slight gradient fade for your background to make your background more appealing but only if the gradient is subtle and not too distracting.

In the sample slide by Pankaj Ghemawat (*www.AkashKaria.com/Pankaj*), who presented at the TED Global 2012, Pankaj uses a simple black background. Check out the sample slide:

Source: Pankaj Ghemawat via TED

The reason Pankaj's slide works well is because he has a clean black background that allows the audience to focus on the statistic that he is presenting. In addition, the text is white. This creates a great contrast that makes the text easily readable.

According to Garr Reynolds, the author of Presentation Zen (*www.PresentationZen.com*):

"If you will be presenting in a dark room (such as a large hall), then a dark background (dark blue, grey, etc.) with white or light text will work fine. But if you plan to keep most of the lights on (which is highly advisable) then a white background with black or dark text works much better. In rooms with a good deal of ambient light, a screen image with a dark background and light text tends to washout, but dark text on a light background will maintain its visual intensity a bit better."

When creating your TED slides, always ensure that there is sufficient contrast between your background and the text. If you are using a dark background, use a light color for your font. If you are using a light background, use a dark color for your font.

How do you know if there is enough contrast between the background and the text?

Simple.

You should be able to read the text from the back of the room you will be presenting in without having to squint your eyes.

In any case, whatever color scheme you decide to use for the background and the text, make sure you stick to the same color scheme throughout the rest of your presentation so that there is continuity between your slides. If you are unsure about which color scheme to use, check out *www.ColorLovers.com* for inspiration.

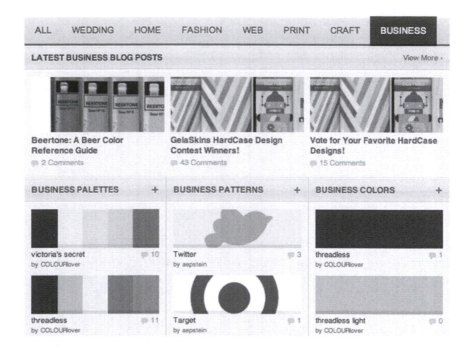

Another great website you can use to create great color themes is Kuler (*http://kuler.adobe.com*). Kuler allows you to upload an image and then generate a color scheme based on the colors used in the image.

USING AN IMAGE AS A BACKGROUND

You don't necessarily have to use a plain background. Sometimes, it can be more visually exciting and appropriate to use an image as a background instead. The picture should fill up the entire slide (with the text being placed upon it), such as in the slide from Bill Gates' TED talk on energy, "Innovating to zero":

Source: Bill Gates via TED

If you do decide to use an image as a background, make sure that the image is consistent with the text. The image should always complement the message of the slide.

ADD TEXT OVER NON-NOISY SECTIONS OF THE IMAGE

If you are going to use an image as a background, it's important to keep in mind that images usually have noisy and non-noisy sections. The noisy section of an image refers to the part of the image where there is a lot going on. In other words, there are a lot of visual elements and colors in that part of the image.

111

If you want to ensure sufficient contrast between the text and the background, ensure that you place your text over the non-noisy sections of the image. As an example, check out this sample slide that I created for one of my presentations:

Source: Akash Karia

In this image, you can see that the text has been positioned over the non-noisy elements of the image. For example, the words "Public Speaking" have been placed at the top of the image because that part of the picture is very "quiet" – there is not much happening there. The blue color of the sky (at least in the color-version of this book!) allows the words to stick out.

Here's another example where the text has been placed over the non-noisy section of the image. This slide is from a TED talk by Dan Pallato (*www.AkashKaria.com/Pallato*):

Source: Dan Pallato via TED

So, where can you find images with enough quiet space for you to be able to place your text?

One resource is iStockphoto's CopySpace.

Here's how to locate beautiful photos with enough breathing space for you to place your text:

1. Go to *www.istockphoto.com/search*.

2. Scroll down until you see the CopySpace function on the left-hand side of your screen.

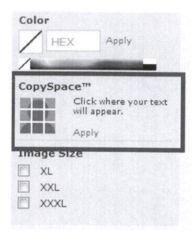

3. Click on the areas of the image where your text will appear (in other words, areas of the photo which you want to remain quiet/blank).

4. Enter a keyword that represents what you are looking for.

After you hit the search button, this will generate images which fit your keyword and which contain enough quiet space for you to be able to position your text.

If you need any more help on how to use iStockphoto's CopySpace function, you can find detailed instructions here: *http://www.istockphoto.com/copyspace_guide.php*

When designing your presentations, use images that contain enough quiet space for you to be able to position the text over. Your image should contain a healthy balance of noisy and quiet sections so that the slide doesn't feel too cluttered.

ADD COLOR TO THE TEXT BOX

What if your image has no quiet space for you to place your text over? What if, no matter what font color you choose, there is not enough contrast between your text and the background to make your font readable? For example, consider the following slide:

Source: Akash Karia / Image on slide: Paul Bica via Flickr

In the slide above, the picture is too busy, making it difficult to achieve sufficient contrast between the text and the image.

One option to achieve better contrast is to fill the text box with color. For example, we could fill the text box with a black background. After filling the text box with a dark background and choosing a contrasting font color, this is how the slide would look:

Source: Akash Karia | Image on slide: Paul Bica via Flickr

After filling the text box with color, the text is now readable.

Another option to achieve the same effect is to place a shape (such as a box or a circle) behind the text and to fill the shape with color.

Here's an example of how such a slide would look (taken from Bill Gates' TED talk, "Teachers need real feedback", which you can view here: *www.AkashKaria.com/Gates*). Notice how a "speech-box" has been placed behind the text in order to make the text stand out:

Source: Bill Gates via TED

Here's another example from Jesse Desjardins' popular presentation, "You suck at PowerPoint!" (*http://bit.ly/18YRJwU*):

Source: Jesse Desjardins via Slideshare

Another option is to fill the text box (or shape) with a solid color but to make it semi-transparent, such as:

Source: Akash Karia / Image on slide: Paul Bica via Flickr

To make a text box (or shape) semi-transparent, go to *Format Shape >> Fill >> Transparency.* Use the transparency slider to make your shape as transparent as you wish.

Making the text box semi-transparent allows the background image to still be visible while ensuring sufficient contrast between the text and the background so that your text is readable.

Here's an example of a slide from a TED talk by Tim Leberecht (*www.AkashKaria.com/TimTalk*) that uses a semi-transparent box to make the text readable:

Semco: Set the salary

Source: Tim Leberecht via TED

Here's one final example (next page). This one comes from Wolfgang Kessling's TED talk on "How to air-condition outdoor spaces" (*www.AkashKaria.com/Wolfgang*).

In this slide, the text box has been filled with a white color (instead of black) and been made semi-transparent:

Source: Wolfgang Kessling via TED

IN A NUTSHELL

- Ensure sufficient contrast between the background and the text.

- Consider using an image as the background and filling the non-noisy sections with text.

- Use semi-transparent text boxes to make your text readable against busy backgrounds.

CHAPTER ELEVEN

DISPLAYING DATA WITHOUT BEING DULL

Examples:

- *Julian Treasure*
- *Bill Gates*
- *Guy Kawasaki*
- *Ethos3*
- *Nic Marks*

Visuals help improve information clarity and retention. Slides are very useful for displaying graphs, charts and other types of data. However, most presenters simply do a data-dump on their slides, throwing lots of tables, graphs and charts onto the slide without much thought regarding the effectiveness of doing so.

Here are some tested principles for designing effective charts and graphs:

MAKE YOUR STATS LARGE AND BOLD

If you're going to be displaying statistics on screen, make sure they are large and impactful. For example, consider how in his TED talk, "Why architects need to use their ears" (*www.AkashKaria.com/Julian*), Julian Treasure filled up his entire slide with a statistic:

Source: Julian Treasure via TED

The large, bold statistic draws attention to it, which then allows Julian to elaborate on the statistic and what it means.

Here's another example, taken from Bill Gates' TED talk, "Teachers need real feedback":

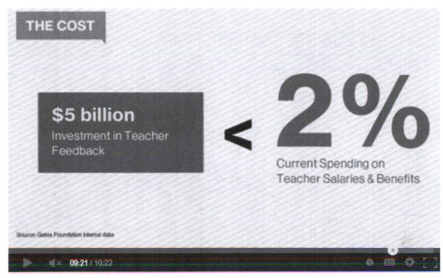

Source: Bill Gates via TED

Again, notice how the main statistic is large and easily visible from the back of the room.

COMBINE STATISTICS WITH PICTURES

One powerful way to make your statistics even more interesting is to combine them with pictures. For example, if you're talking about global warming and want to use the statistic that "in 20 years, our icecaps will be melted," then you could place the statistic on top of the image of icecaps melting.

Here's an example from Bill Gates' TED talk on energy, where he places the digit zero (along with text) on an image of the Earth taken from space:

Source: Bill Gates via TED

Turn the page and you'll see an example from Bill Gates' TED talk. Notice how the statistic, "Paducah, Kentucky, has enough uranium to power the US for two centuries," is made much more interesting as a result of having been placed on an image that shows thousands of uranium barrels:

Combining statistics with images has several advantages. It:

- Makes the slide more visually appealing.
- Helps the audience interpret the significance and meaning of the statistic.
- Makes the statistic more memorable.

Consider using a visually stunning image as the backdrop upon which you place your statistic. The image you use will impact how your audience interprets the statistic, so make sure you use an image that tells the story you want it to.

ONE STATISTIC, ONE SLIDE

Look at the following slide. How interesting is it? Does it grab your attention? Does it want to make you know more?

Number of weeks from registering truemors.com to launching it	7.5
Cost of software development	$4500
Cost of legal fees	$4824.13

Source: Akash Karia/ Statistics on slide: Guy Kawasaki

I don't know about you, but the above slide completely fails to engage me.

Now, consider the slides featured in the next couple of pages, which present the same statistics in a much more visually engaging manner. These slides were taken from Guy Kawasaki's presentation (designed by presentation-design company *Ethos3*) on how he launched *http://www.Truemors.com*

128

Consider how much more effective the following slides are compared to the table on the previous page:

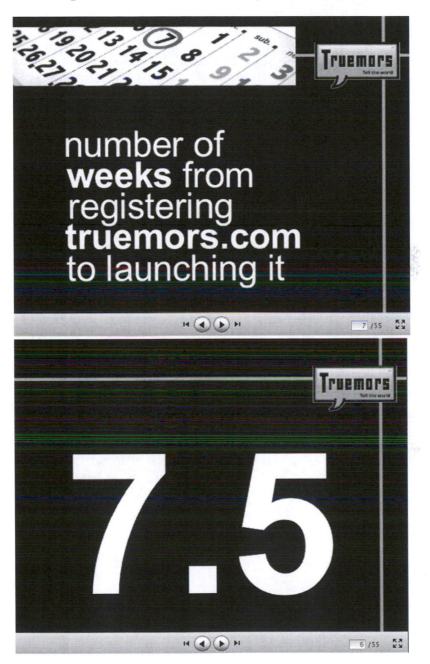

Slides: Guy Kawasaki via Ethos 3

Tables are great for comparing data, but if you don't need to compare two data points against each other, then consider displaying each statistic on its own slide.

USE IMAGES TO DIRECT YOUR AUDIENCE'S EYES TO THE DATA

If you're going to be pairing pictures up with text, use images that guide your audience's eyes towards the text (or data).

Our eyes are naturally drawn to images first, and then follow the image from the focal point to the end point of the image.

Make sure that when your audience's eyes reach the end point of the image, they are looking at a piece of data/text. This way, you manage to naturally guide your audience's eyes.

Here's an example:

Slide: Akash Karia / Image on slide: MikeBaird via Compfight

Notice how the image above helps guide the audience's eyes from the picture to the statistic. The jogger is running towards the statistic – causing the audience's eyes to naturally move towards it.

USE APPROPRIATE CHARTS

It's important to make sure that you use the right type of chart for the right data. I won't dive into a math lesson here, but it's important to make sure that the type of chart/graph you choose to display is the best type for displaying the information.

For example, if you were giving a presentation to the CEO and wanted to compare how much revenue each product brought in, a pie chart would be a better option than a table.

Why?

Because a pie chart would allow your audience to quickly decipher what percentage of the company's income was generated from each product, whereas it would take longer for your audience to get the same information from a table.

Here are some of the best practices to keep in mind when using different types of graphs and charts.

PIE CHARTS

Pie charts are great for displaying percentages. Two important things to keep in mind: First, limit the number of slices in the pie chart to less than six, otherwise the whole pie chart can look too crowded, making it harder for your audience to absorb information.

Here's an example (on the next page) of a simple and effective pie chart from Bill Gates' TED talk (*www.AkashKaria.com/BillGates*) on "How the state budgets are breaking US schools":

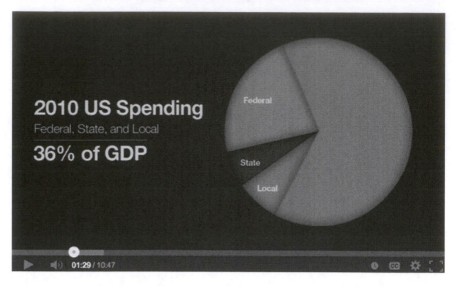

Source: Bill Gates via TED

VERTICAL BAR CHARTS

Vertical bar charts are great for changes in quantity over time.

Again, it's best to limit the amount of data your audience has to absorb by limiting the number of bars on your chart to less than six.

Here's an example of a clear bar chart from Nic Marks' TED talk (*www.AkashKaria.com/Nic*), "The happy planet index":

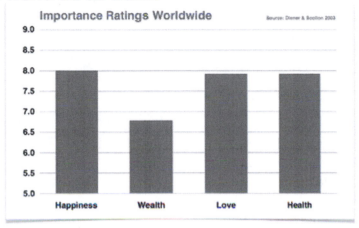

Source: Nic Marks via TED

A great technique you can use is to draw attention to a particular bar by having it a different color than the rest. This sends a clear message to your audience regarding what they should be focusing on.

Check out an example slide (next page) from Bill Gates' TED talk (*www.AkashKaria.com/BillGates*) on education:

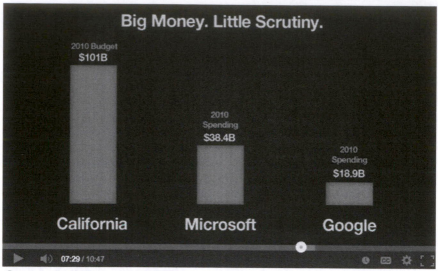

Source: Bill Gates via TED

LINE CHARTS

Line charts are mainly used to display trends over time.

The important thing to keep in mind when using line charts is that the line should be easily visible from the back of the room.

This means that the line needs to be thick enough to be seen from afar, as well as set against a plain contrasting background (turn the page):

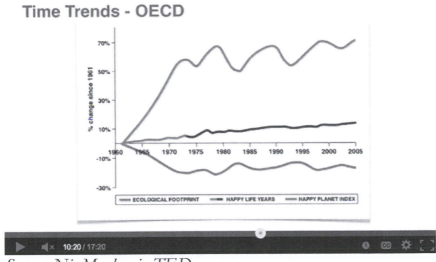

Source: *Nic Marks via TED*

Here's another example from Bill Gates' TED talk:

Source: *Bill Gates via TED*

While there are many more methods of displaying data, pie charts, vertical bar charts and line charts are among the three most common ones.

However, no matter which type of graph or chart you choose to display your data, make sure that the type you choose is the most appropriate one for conveying your point clearly. Furthermore, make sure that the chart is simple, clear, readable, clutter-free and easy to understand.

LABEL EVERYTHING CLEARLY

When displaying graphs and data, make sure that you label everything clearly. The labels should be large and visible from the back of the room. If your audience has to squint to make sense of your graphs, they're going to stop trying and tune out of your presentation.

BUILD UP COMPLICATED GRAPHS AND CHARTS

According to the guidelines on the TEDx speaker guide, you should "keep graphs visually clear, even if the content is complex. Each graph should make only one point."

However, sometimes – not very often, but sometimes – a diagram might be very complicated and might require you to make more than one point. What do you do in this case?

If your graph or chart has too many elements, it is best to build it up element by element. For example, if you had a very complicated line chart with several different lines, you would display the first line, explain it, then display the second one, explain it, etc. This way, you're building the line chart up in a logical, systematic way that allows your audience to comprehend it without being overwhelmed.

IN A NUTSHELL

- Make your statistics large and bold.

- Combine statistics with images.

- Use images to direct audience's eyes towards the data.

- Label graphs and charts clearly.

- Use builds to make complicated graphs and charts easier to digest.

CHAPTER TWELVE

SPICING UP YOUR PRESENTATIONS WITH VIDEO

Examples:

- *Amy Cuddy*

Research shows that audience attention drops considerably after ten minutes of listening to a presentation. This means that it's important to change things up within your presentation. If you're talking to your audience nonstop for ten minutes, perhaps try having some audience involvement to increase your audience's attention levels.

Alternatively, you can play a video to change things up and keep your audiences engaged. In her TED talk on body language, Amy Cuddy made great use of embedded videos within her presentation.

Videos are great because:

- **They provide a change of pace.** This change of pace results in a spike in audience attention, and when your audiences do come back to listening to you, attention levels are higher than they were before the video.

- **They allow you to quickly show what would take a long time to describe.** If you were trying to describe a very complicated experiment or setup, then sometimes it might be better to show a 30-second video as opposed to spending three minutes trying to explain it.

- **They can be more powerful than pictures.** Pictures are great, but videos are more powerful because they involve and engage all the senses. As an example, when I see a picture of the plane crashing into the Twin Towers on 9/11, I can recall what a tragic incident that was. However, when I see a 30-second video of the plane crashing into the towers, it still leaves me in shock.

Whether you decide to use a video to provide a change of pace or stir your audience's emotions, keep in mind the following principles:

- **Keep it short.** Keep your videos relatively short. For a TED talk, where you are given only 18 minutes, it's best to keep the length of your videos to less than 30 seconds. Remember, your audience is there to see you, not your video. So use the video to make a point, but keep the video short.

- **Make sure the video is high quality.** The last thing you want is a pixelated video playing on the screen.

- **Embed the video into your presentation.** Have you ever seen a speaker minimize the presentation so that he could fumble around on the desktop looking for the right file to play?

- Unfortunately, I've seen too many speakers do this. Even though it may only take the speaker a couple of seconds to locate the file, this interrupts the flow and continuity of the presentation. The speaker appears unprepared and unorganized, and the audience stops paying attention to him and starts talking among themselves.

- The solution to this is very simple: Embed the video file into the presentation. To embed a video into a presentation, simply go to *Insert >> Movie/Video >> Movie/Video from file:*

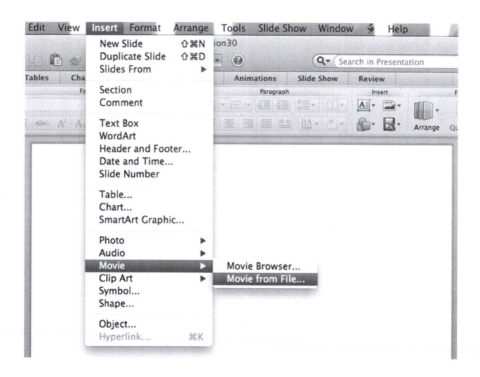

IN A NUTSHELL

- Keep your video short.

- Use high-quality video.

- Embed the video into your presentation.

CHAPTER THIRTEEN

"HOW DO I MAKE IT ALL CONSISTENT?"

Examples:

- *Sebastian Wernicke*
- *Jesse Desjardins*
- *Eugene Cheng*

It's important that your slides have some kind of consistent look and feel to them. There has to be some kind of unifying element that weaves all the slides together so that your slides do not look like a series of random, disjointed photos with text on them.

How do you add consistency to your slides?

FONT CONSISTENCY

The first and most obvious way is to make sure that you use the same font combination for all the slides. Whatever combination of the fonts you decide to use for your first slide, make sure you stick to the same combination throughout the rest of your slides.

For example, check out how Sebastian Wernicke uses the same font throughout his entire TED presentation in order to create consistency between the slides (*www.AkashKaria.com/Sebastian*):

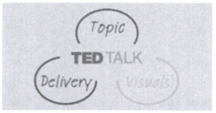 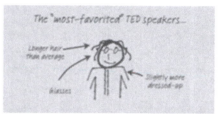

Source: Sebastian Wernicke via TED

IMAGE STYLE CONSISTENCY

A second way is to use images that are similar in style.

For example, consider how the presentation designer Jesse Desjardins used a collection of black-and-white images with a similar style to create a unified theme for his presentation (*http://bit.ly/18YRJwU*):

You can also make use of icons and symbols to create a unifying theme for your presentation.

For example, look at how Eugene Cheng (*www.ItsEugene.me*) used icons in the following slides to create consistency:

VISUAL ELEMENT CONSISTENCY

A third method is to have a visual element in your slide that is repeated consistently throughout your slides. For example, consider the slides by Eugene Cheng on the next few pages.

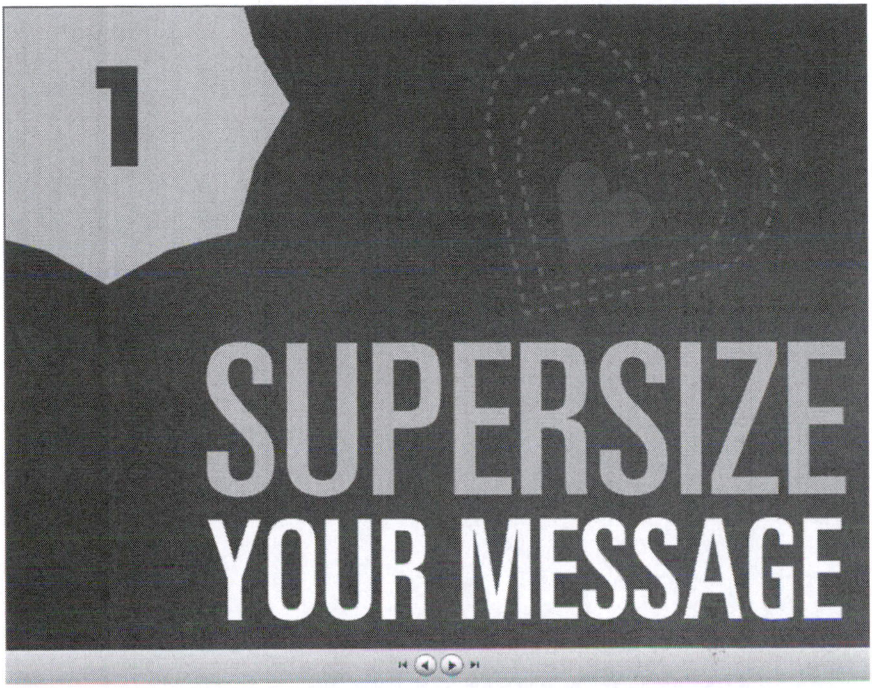
1
SUPERSIZE
YOUR MESSAGE

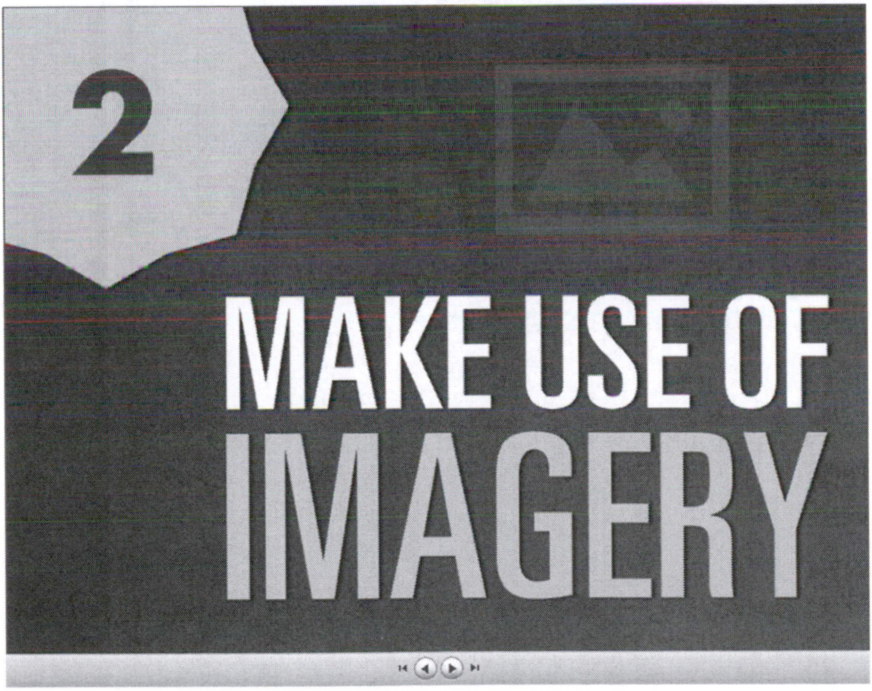
2
MAKE USE OF
IMAGERY

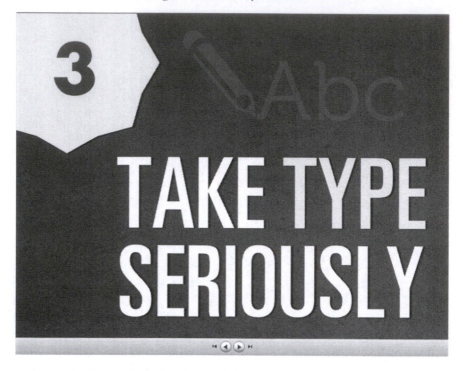

The previous three slides are visually consistent because:

- The background is the same for all the slides.
- The same fonts are used through all three slides.
- All slides are numbered with a half-octagon shape in the top left-hand side of the slide that appears throughout all the slides.

When creating your slides, aim for visual consistency between the slides. This creates a sense of unity between the slides and leads to a more harmonious slide deck that flows easily from one slide to the next.

IN A NUTSHELL

To make your slides consistent and create a sense of continuity between them, ensure:

- Font consistency.

- Image style consistency.

- Visual element consistency.

PART 3

YOUR DELIVERY

- How to prepare for your talk
- How to deliver a great TED talk
- Wrap up

CHAPTER FOURTEEN

HOW TO PREPARE FOR YOUR TED TALK

Now that you've prepared your slides for your talk, it's time to start preparing for the big day. Here are several tips that will help you learn how to flawlessly interact with your slides:

1. PRACTICE YOUR PRESENTATION WITH SLIDES

It's important that you rehearse your presentation with your slides because that will give you a huge confidence boost during your talk. Practice how you will explain each slide. Practice the transitions between slides. This will also help you catch any problems you might have when speaking with slides.

For example, there have been several times in my career as a professional speaker when, after having storyboarded and prepared my slides, I came to the rehearsal phase of the talk and realized that a certain slide just wasn't working – either it wasn't needed, or it needed to be moved to a later part of the presentation. Practice your presentation out loud so that you get used to working with your slides.

When it comes to rehearsing your presentation, there are several rehearsal strategies that work best for me:

- **Practice out loud.** Find an empty room and practice your presentation out loud so that your mouth gets used to saying what your mind wants it to say.

- **Practice at normal speed.** Practice your talk at your normal speaking pace, the way you would as if you were delivering it in front of an actual audience. Take longer pauses where you expect your audience to be laughing so that you get used to being silent on stage.

- **Practice at double the speed.** Go through your presentation at twice the speed that you would normally speak at. You should finish your presentation in half the time it would normally take. Doing this helps you solidify the presentation structure in your mind.

- **Practice at half your speaking pace.** Deliberately slow down to half your normal speaking pace. This

will feel uncomfortable but it will work wonders in helping you internalize your talk.

- **Practice mentally.** Apart from practicing out loud, it's important that you practice mentally. Mentally go through what you will say and how you will say it.

- **Practice in chunks.** If it's too much to practice your presentation in one go, then practice it in chunks. In the morning, practice your opening; in the afternoon practice your first point; at night practice your closing. By practicing in chunks, you manage to internalize all parts of your talk equally.

- **Practice in front of a live audience.** Organize a rehearsal night with your friends and family. Invite your friends to watch you give a live presentation. This will help you get used to speaking when people are watching you. It will also allow you to judge audience reactions – did they laugh at points where you expected them to laugh? Did they understand what you were saying or did they seem confused?

- Ask your friends and family members to give you feedback on how you can improve. Say, "I want to know what I can do better. Please give me at least one point of improvement." Get people to anonymously fill out feedback forms and give you a rating on a scale of 0 to 10 (with 0 being terrible and 10 being perfect).

2. ARRIVE EARLY AND TEST THE EQUIPMENT

Arrive early at the venue and practice (if possible) delivering your presentation from the stage. This will get you comfortable with speaking from the stage and will reduce your nervousness when you do get up to deliver your talk in front of the audience. Test all the equipment and ensure that your slides display as intended.

3. WHAT TO AVOID

Avoid speaking on a full stomach because your body will focus its energy on digesting your food. Avoid eating two hours before your talk. Instead, have a cookie or a sweet before your talk to give you the energy you need for your talk. Also, avoid caffeine because it will result in a dry mouth during your speech.

4. SIT IN ALL FOUR CORNERS OF THE ROOM

Sit in all four corners of the room so that you get a sense of how you will appear from the back of the room. Make sure your slides are visible from the back.

5. GET TO KNOW YOUR AUDIENCE MEMBERS

Network with your audience members. Meet as many people as you can. This will help you develop a connection with them even before you get up on stage.

6. VISUALIZE

Right before your talk, take some time to yourself. Get away from everyone else so that you can focus on your talk. Visualize yourself giving your talk. Visualize yourself opening and closing powerfully. Visualize yourself making a difference in someone's life because of your talk.

7. ACCEPT IT WON'T BE PERFECT

Positive visualizations work, but they have a downside. If you expect that everything will be easy – that your talk will go flawlessly and nothing will go wrong – then you will be putting too much pressure on yourself. And, when things will wrong – which they will – you will be too flustered and shocked to handle them well. Instead of seeking perfection, accept that you will make some mistakes and you will stumble over your words. This will remove pressure off you, and ironically, this will result in a more authentic and powerful presentation.

IN A NUTSHELL

- Practice your presentation with slides.

- Arrive early to test the equipment.

- Sit in all four corners of the room.

- Get to know your audience members.

- Visualize.

- Accept your talk won't be perfect.

CHAPTER FIFTEEN

HOW TO DELIVER A GREAT TED TALK

The aim of this short guide has been to show you how to design effective slides, but I feel that this guide would be incomplete without at least a couple of words on how to use your slides to deliver your message.

DON'T READ YOUR SLIDES

One of the most common mistakes I see most presenters make is that they read their slides word for word. If you've followed the advice on limiting the amount of text on your slides to just keywords, this will ensure that you don't fall victim to the trap of reading your slides.

However, it bears repeating that you shouldn't read your slides. Instead of simply reading the words on the slide, elaborate on each point. Make your presentation interesting using examples and personal stories.

Remember, your audience is there to see and listen to *you*, so keep the focus on you, not on your slides. You are the star, not your slides.

PROVIDE VERBAL TRANSITIONS BETWEEN SLIDES

One mistake I see many presenters make is that they have no verbal transitions between their slides. In other words, they will talk about a slide, then pause, click the next one, and start talking about that one. The effect of this is that your presentation lacks a continuity and flow.

A better way to do this would be to have verbal transitions between your slides. Yes, this requires you to know which slide is coming up next, but if you've practiced your presentation (which you should have), then this should not be a problem. The right way to transition between your slides is to start introducing the concept in the next slide using a transition statement.

Let me give you an example. Let's say that I was giving a presentation on the effects of global warming. On the next page, you can see two sample slides from my hypothetical presentation:

Slide 1: Akash Karia / Image on slide: Christine Zenino

Slide 2: Akash Karia / Image on slide: IceSabre

In slide 1, I would explain the negative consequences of global warming. Then, before I click on the next slide, I would say, "So, is there anything we can do to stop global warming?" This is my transition statement and introduces my next slide before it comes up. This way, instead of seeming like a disjointed presentation, my presentation has a certain continuity and flow to it.

LET YOUR PASSION FLOW

One of the things that I've noticed is that people who use slides to present are usually very mechanical and robotic in their delivery. This isn't true of all the speakers, but from what I've seen, it's generally true.

On the other hand, speakers who speak without slides are usually more passionate and dynamic when speaking. Why is this? It could be that people who choose to speak without slides are simply better presenters and more confident in their ability to speak in public.

However, I've also noticed that when I speak without PowerPoint, I usually am a lot more energetic than when I do speak using slides.

Why?

I have a theory that speakers who present using slides have activated the logical, analytical parts of their brains, which makes them very mechanical in their delivery.

Speakers who speak without slides do not have to think about the logical transitions between one slide and the next, and as a result, they are able to let their emotions flow when they speak.

So, what does this have to do with delivering powerful TED talks?

A TED talk is not a mechanical recitation of your points. It's your opportunity to share your message and your passion with the world. You've been given 18 minutes to share your message with the world.

Even though you are using slides, this does not mean that your delivery needs to be mechanical. Let your passion and your excitement flow through when you speak. Be excited about what you're sharing. Instead of focusing on your slides, focus on your audience. Let your excitement about the topic flow through to your audience. When you are passionate and excited about what you're sharing, your audience will be too.

FORGET ABOUT YOURSELF

During an interview I conducted for my blog with public speaking champion Lisa Panarello, I asked her, "What is the most important public speaking tip you've learned?" She replied: "Forget about you."

What does it mean to forget about yourself? It means to stop focusing on how you look and how you sound. Don't focus on how you're dressed, how you sound and how your slides look.

Instead, focus 100% on your audience. Focus on the message that you are sharing with them. Focus on your *why* for delivering the message. Focus on the change you want to create in your audience.

When you forget about yourself and about your slides, you will find that your nervousness will disappear. Instead of feeling self-conscious, you will feel totally confident because you're focused on your audience and not on yourself.

When you focus on your audience, you will build an unbreakable connection with your audience and you will deliver a powerful and dynamic talk.

IN A NUTSHELL

- Don't read your slides.

- Provide verbal transitions between slides.

- Let your passion flow.

- Forget about yourself.

CHAPTER 16

WRAP-UP: HOW TO CREATE TED-WORTHY SLIDES

You've watched and analysed the slides of some of the best presenters on the planet. You've learned how to create effective, visually appealing slides that help breathe life into your message. Because there are so many tools covered in this tiny book, this chapter will serve as a useful checklist when you start creating your next presentation slide deck.

Here's a quick list of all the presentation design tools covered in this book. I suggest that you come back and read this list several weeks later to refresh your memory:

1. Start with your core message.

2. Create an audience-centred presentation.

3. Resist the temptation to start creating your slides immediately. Instead, do an idea-dump on a piece of paper to get your thoughts and points clear.

4. Limit the amount of text on your slide. Remember, the aim is to create a visually appealing slide, not a slideument.

5. Make sure each slide contains only one idea.

6. Use as many slides as you need. There is no rule that you need to limit the number of slides in your presentation.

7. Follow the Seth Godin presentation formula. Fill your slides with large images and very little or no text.

8. Ask yourself, "How can this idea be represented visually?"

9. Use images that create an emotional response in your audience.

10. Use high-quality digital photos from quality stock photo sites. Alternatively, if you are a photographer, use high-resolution pictures that you have taken.

11. Full bleed images. Use visually stunning images that fill up the entire slide.

12. Think of your slides as billboards. The main message of your slide should be clear to your audience within three seconds or less.

13. Follow the rule of thirds to create more interesting images.

14. Avoid clichéd images. Look for fresh, new and unique ways to represent your idea visually.

15. Learn to appreciate empty space.

16. Use large, sexy fonts to make your slides visually engaging.

17. Choose a font that matches your message.

18. Stick to a maximum of two font types.

19. Design for the person sitting at the back of the room.

20. Vary font size to create excitement.

21. Pay attention to alignment.

22. Experiment with rotating text.

23. Ensure sufficient contrast between the image and the text.

24. Add text over non-noisy sections of the image.

25. If you have a very busy image, use semi-transparent text boxes to make your text readable.

26. Ensure the fonts, images and visual elements in your presentation are consistent throughout the presentation.

27. Use the appropriate chart for representing your data.

28. Label your charts and graphs clearly.

29. Incorporate builds into your charts and graphs if necessary.

30. Provide verbal transitions between slides

31. When delivering your presentation, don't read your slides. Speak with energy and enthusiasm. Let your passion flow. Forget about yourself. Focus on your audience.

QUESTIONS OR COMMENTS?

I'd love to hear your thoughts. Email me at:
akash.speaker@gmail.com

INTERESTED IN HAVING ME SPEAK AT YOUR NEXT EVENT?

I deliver high-impact keynotes and workshops on productivity, time-management, success psychology and effective communication. Check out the full list of my training programs on http://AkashKaria.com/keynotes/ and reach me on akash.speaker@gmail.com to discuss how we can work together.

GRAB $297 WORTH OF FREE RESOURCES

Want to learn the small but powerful hacks to make you insanely productive? Want to discover the scientifically proven techniques to ignite your influence? Interested in mastering the art of public speaking and charisma? Then head over to http://www.AkashKaria.com to grab your free "10X Success Toolkit" (free MP3s, eBooks and videos designed to unleash your excellence). Be sure to sign up for the newsletter and join over 11,800 of your peers to receive free, exclusive content that I don't share on my blog.

YOU MIGHT ALSO ENJOY

If you enjoyed this book, then check out Akash's other books (and see what other readers are saying).

HOW TO DELIVER A GREAT TED TALK: PRESENTATION SECRETS OF THE WORLD'S BEST SPEAKERS

"Why can some speakers grab the attention of an audience and keep them spellbound throughout their entire presentation, but most fall flat on their faces and are quickly forgotten? Akash has captured the best ideas, tools, and processes used by some of the best speakers and presenters in the world. He has distilled them in to a step-by-step, easy-to-read guide that will help you discover, develop, and deliver presentations which help you stand out from the crowd…Whether you are a new speaker learning the art of speaking, or a veteran looking for a new perspective, How to Deliver a Great TED Talk is a wise investment that can help take your speaking to a higher level."
~ Michael Davis, Certified World Class Speaking Coach

"I waited quite a while to read this book, and now that I have, I wish I would have opened it sooner. Fantastic information and easy to follow format."
~ Noell Beadelia

Get the book on Amazon:
http://AkashKaria.com/TEDTalkBook/

179

ANTI NEGATIVITY: HOW TO STOP NEGATIVE THINKING AND LEAD A POSITIVE LIFE

"Akash is a master at taking complex ideas and communicating with simplicity and brilliance. He honors your time by presenting what you need to know right away, and follows up with some excellent examples as reinforcement. If you're looking for some simple and effective ways to stop thinking negatively and a new season of positivity, definitely check out this book."
~ Justin Morgan

Get the book on Amazon:
http://AkashKaria.com/AntiNegativity/

PERSUASION PSYCHOLOGY: 26 POWERFUL TECHNIQUES TO PERSUADE ANYONE!

"I'm a huge fan of Akash's writing style and the way he can distill quite a complex subject into concise bite-sized points you can take away and convert into action. The book covers many different aspects of persuasion from the way you look to the words you use."
~ Rob Cubbon, author of "From Freelancer to Entrepreneur"

Get the book on Amazon:

http://AkashKaria.com/Persuasion/

READY, SET...PROCRASTINATE! 23 ANTI-PROCRASTINATION TOOLS DESIGNED TO HELP YOU STOP PUTTING THINGS OFF AND START GETTING THINGS DONE

"This is one book you should not delay reading! Having struggled with procrastination for much of my life, Akash Karia's book came like a breath of fresh air. He provides clear, practical advice on how to overcome the problem, but warns that you will need to work at it daily. This is a quick, very useful read and with 23 tips on offer, there will be several that you can identify with and implement for immediate results. If there is just one thing that you should not put off, it is reading this book."

~ Gillian Findlay

Get the book on Amazon:
http://AkashKaria.com/AntiProcrastination/

WANT MORE?

Then check out Akash's author-page on Amazon:
http://bit.ly/AkashKaria

ABOUT THE AUTHOR

Akash Karia is an award winning speaker and peak-productivity coach who has been ranked as one of the Top Ten speakers in Asia Pacific. He is an in-demand international speaker who has spoken to a wide range of audiences including bankers in Hong Kong, students in Tanzania, governmental organizations in Dubai and yoga teachers in Thailand. He currently lives in Tanzania where he works as the Chief Commercial Officer of a multi-million dollar company.

"If you want to learn presentation skills, public speaking or just simply uncover excellence hidden inside of you or your teams, **Akash Karia is the coach to go to.**" ~ *Raju Mandhyan, TV show host, Expat Insights, Philippines*

"Akash Karia is a fine public speaker who knows his subject very well. He has an immense understanding in what it takes for a successful presentation to pull through. **A rare talent who has much in store for you as an individual, and better yet, your organization.**" ~ *Sherilyn Pang, Business Reporter, Capital TV, Malaysia*

Voted as one of the "**10 online entrepreneurs you need to know in 2015**" by *The Expressive Leader*

Featured as one of the "**top 9 [online] presentations of 2014**" by *AuthorStream.com*

Akash is available for speaking engagements and flies from Tanzania. Contact him for coaching and training through his website: www.AkashKaria.com

TED TALKS REFERENCED

For your convenience, here's a list of the TED Talks (*www.TED.com*) analyzed in this book (in alphabetical order):

Al Gore
"Averting the climate crisis"
www.AkashKaria.com/Gore

Speaker's website:
www.AlGore.com

Amy Cuddy
"Your body language shapes who you are"
www.AkashKaria.com/Amy

Speaker's website:
www.People.hbs.edu/ACuddy

Bill Gates
"Innovating to zero!"
www.AkashKaria.com/Bill

"Teachers need real feedback"
www.AkashKaria.com/Gates

How state budgets are breaking US schools
www.AkashKaria.com/BillGates

Speaker's website:
www.GatesNotes.com

Brene Brown
"The power of vulnerability"
www.AkashKaria.com/Brene

Speaker's website:
www.BreneBrown.com

Daniel Pink
"The puzzle of motivation"
www.AkashKaria.com/Dan

Speaker's website:
www.DanPink.com

George Papandreou
"Imagine a European
democracy without borders"
www.AkashKaria.com/George

Speaker's website:
www.Papandreou.gr/en

Julian Treasure
"Why architects need to use
their ears"
www.AkashKaria.com/Julian

Speaker's website:
www.JulianTreasure.com

Nancy Duarte
"The secret structure of great
TED talks"
www.AkashKaria.com/Nancy

Speaker's website:
www.Duarte.com

Dan Pallato
"The way we think about
charity is dead wrong"
www.AkashKaria.com/Pallato

Speaker's Website:
www.DanPallotta.com

Jacqueline Novogratz
"An escape from poverty"
www.AkashKaria.com/Jacqueline

Speaker's website:
www.Acumen.org/Bluesweater

Larry Lessig
"Laws that choke creativity"
www.AkashKaria.com/Larry

Speaker's website:
www.Lessig.org

Nic Marks
"The happy planet index"
www.AkashKaria.com/Nic

Speaker's website:
www.NicMarks.org

Nilofer Merchant
"Got a meeting? Take a walk"
www.AkashKaria.com/Nilofer

Speaker's Website:
www.NiloferMerchant.com

Paul Kemp-Robertson
"Bitcoin. Sweat. Tide. Meet the future of branded currency."
www.AkashKaria.com/Paul

Speaker's website:
www.Contagious.com

Sebastian Wernicke
"Lies, damned lies and statistics (about TEDTalks)"
www.AkashKaria.com/Sebastian

Speaker's website:
www.Get-TedPad.com

Simon Sinek
"How great leaders inspire action"
www.AkashKaria.com/Simon

Speaker's website:
www.StartWithWhy.com

Pankaj Ghemawat
"Actually, the world isn't flat"
www.AkashKaria.com/Pankaj

Speaker's website:
www.Ghemawat.com

Rachel Botsman
"The currency of the new economy is trust."
www.AkashKaria.com/Rachel

Speaker's website:
www.RachelBotsman.com

Seth Godin
"The tribes we lead"
www.AkashKaria.com/Seth

Speaker's website:
www.SethGodin.com

Sir Ken Robinson
"Do schools kill creativity?"
www.AkashKaria.com/Ken

Speaker's website:
www.SirKenRobinson.com

Stuart Firestein
"The pursuit of ignorance"
www.AkashKaria.com/Stuart

Speaker's website:
http://bit.ly/StuartFirestein

Wolfgang Kessling
"How to air-condition
outdoor spaces"
www.AkashKaria.com/Wolfgang

Speaker's website:
www.TransSolar.com

Tim Leberecht
"3 ways to (usefully) lose
control of your brand"
www.AkashKaria.com/TimTalk

Speaker's website:
www.TimLeberecht.com

PRESENTATION EXPERTS REFERENCED

Alex Rister
www.AlexRister1.wordpress.com

Carmine Gallo
www.CarmineGallo.com

Darren Rowse
www.ProBlogger.net

Dr. John Medina
www.JohnMedina.com

Ethos3
www.Ethos3.com

Garr Reynols
www.PresentationZen.com

Jesse Desjardins
www.slideshare.net/jessedee

Nancy Duarte
www.Duarte.com

Nilofer Merchant
www.NiloferMerchant.com

Steve Farnsworth
www.SteveFarnsworth.wordpress.com

Becky Blanton
www.BeckyBlanton.com

Chiara Ojeda
www.slideshare.net/ohmgrrl

Douglas Kruger
www.DouglasKruger.com

Emiland de Cubber
www.Emiland.me

Eugene Cheng
www.ItsEugene.me

Guy Kawasaki
www.GuyKawasaki.com

Lisa Panarello
www.CareersAdvance.org

Nick Morgan
www.PublicWords.com

Slides that Rock
www.SlidesThatRock.com

CONNECT WITH AKASH

Get your Free Success Toolkit on:

www.AkashKaria.com

Check out More Awesome Books:

www.bit.ly/AkashKaria

Email for Speaking-Related Inquires:

akash@akashkaria.com / akash.speaker@gmail.com

Connect on Facebook:

www.facebook.com/PublicSpeakingCoach

Connect on LinkedIn:

www.LinkedIn.com/In/AkashKaria

Made in the USA
Middletown, DE
01 October 2015